Howdy, welcome to the Oregon Coast Bike Route!

Get ready to ride ...

OREGON COAST BIKE ROUTE

RIDING THE LEGEND

a cyclist's guide
by steve greene

"True adventure cannot be planned. Rather, it is to be found simply by setting off for the unknown, and then figuring out how to survive along the way."

– Steve Greene

COVER PHOTOS:

Main Cover Spread: Amanda Alexander pedals south along the Oregon Coast Bike Route on an overcast day, looking for a camp. **Rear Cover**: David Massey and Matt Jensen near Sunset Bay, heading for the Seven Devils. A typical Oregon Coast Bike Route Sign as seen the entire way. An impressive sea stack south of Cape Sebastian.

An **OCBR** bike shop list appears on page 315.

the small print cure for insomnia
This book is intended to assist you in using a human powered bicycle or tricycle to pedal the 383 miles found along the Oregon Coast in the western United States. It is not intended to replace your own common sense, or the advice from casual friends you may think know more than the author. In no event should the reader of these pages use the message found in the contents of this book to override the perceived concerns or fervent demands of a spouse or relative. In the event you suspect a conflict exists between your personal desires and the advice offered by real people in your actual life, it may be best to absolutely ignore what you're about to read, and instead read the stories of others who actually rise to the challenge and ride this demanding route. The author disclaims any liability arising from the reader's use of this book, with a caveat: Be careful out there. Live to tell the tale, because as we all learned from pirates since childhood, dead men tell no tales.

OREGON COAST BIKE ROUTE
ISBN-13: 978-1503326163
ISBN-10: 1503326160
Printed in the USA Charleston, SC

Copyright © 2015 by Steve Greene
All rights reserved.

It was challenging pedaling the Oregon Coast, and exceptionally time consuming preparing all this information for you, so please respect all the blood (banged my shin on the crankarm), sweat (pedaled up all the capes), and tears (none, but it sounded good) behind this manuscript, and if you do need to quote or use a portion of it for some apparently important reason, give some credit to the trike hobo who compiled it all, and, if you don't mind while you're at it, please mention the website:
trikeasylum.wordpress.com
Thanks, and have a blast preparing for your awesome odyssey! BTW: Feel free to copy whatever you need for placing in your panniers while on your ride if you would rather not bring the entire book with you on the journey (books are heavy).

HOBO
BOOK

QUICK REFERENCE

The Legend's Siren Song - 9
How is this book different? - 11
A Word about the Maps - 15
The Seven Adventure Maps - 16
Steep Hilly Intense Terrain - 25
Five Flying Saucers at the Beach - 29
Tsunami Facts - 30
The Coast is Clear ... sometimes - 32
Getting Here and Back Home Again - 33
Mileages Between Places - 34
We begin our journey on the beach - 35
Crazy Guy On A Bike Journal - 36
What's up with Astoria? - 37
Fort Stevens State Park - 39
Wild Bushwhackers Found the Way - 42
The State of Oregonia - 43
Why Oregon Business Loves You - 45
Spit first, or it doesn't count! - 49
Fort Stevens to Cannon Beach - 51
Cannon Beach to Nehalem Bay - 62
Pirates, Galleons, & Buried Treasure! - 70
Nehalem Bay to the Land of Cheese - 72
Tillamook to Pacific City - 82
Pacific City to Lincoln City - 100
Why Cyclists Really Love Oregon - 111
Lincoln City to Newport - 113
Newport to Yachats - 130
Whale Watching Spoken Here - 148
Oregon Coast Geology - 151
Why Live in Yachats? - 153
Yachats to Florence - 154
Is it half-time yet? - 187
Oregon Coast Cycling Ghost - 192
Florence to North Bend - 194
Coos Bay Bridge Alternate Route - 226
North Bend to Cranberry Land - 229
Bandon to Cape Blanco - 251
Wild Winds on the Oregon Coast - 264
Cape Blanco to Gold Beach - 266
Gold Beach to California - 281
California - 304
Raiders of the Lost Crumb - 309
Getting High on the OCBR - 312
Did you do the entire OCBR? - 314
Oregon Coast Bicycle Shops - 315

You will encounter two of these tunnel signs on the OCBR.

Thousands of cyclists live this adventure every year! Join 'em!

A surfer at Ecola State Park, with the haunted Tillamook Rock lighthouse visible off shore! Yaquina Bay Bridge in Newport:

THE LEGEND'S SIREN SONG

In the realm of cycle touring, certain locales reach lofty domains of undisputed popularity, mysteriously beckoning to bicyclists the world over to come experience for themselves the adventure on sacred ground, as thousands before them have long since ridden, and continue to enjoy. We ride across countries, through deserts, over cloud covered mountain ranges, and along mighty oceans. Wherever there is pavement, we find a way to explore it.

Where oceans are concerned, Planet Earth was generous in its allotment of spectacular vistas and unforgettable riding out on the western shores of North America, in what is now known as the state of Oregon. Somehow, as if by precise design and intent of the Cycling Gods, those crafty and mischievous pedal-pushing deities, the 383 miles along this particular coastline have risen to the status of legend with bicyclists, and also a few tricyclists.

Why is this so? Well, to be brief, answering that question is the reason for this bizarre alternative guidebook, as we will ride the Oregon Coast together here, at least in our minds and on this paper, in an attempt to fire up the inborn human desires to know what's really out there, over that next hill and around that next bend in the road. Humans happen to be explorers at heart, and all you need do is give them some wheels, and off they go!

This particular portion of the entire Pacific Coast route of the western United States just happens to be what most riders describe as the most spectacular and scenic of all the miles from Canada to Mexico, thus resulting in the immense popularity that attracts thousands of bicyclists each and every summer season. If we attempt to ride the coast of Washington to the north, much of the time we'll be inland far from the water, and if we ride to the south in California, we'll see plenty of gorgeous ocean and cliffs, but the environment is markedly drier and grassy. Oregon simply stands out as the best of the best, and if you are going to choose a single section of coastline to pedal, this choice is unbeatable!

This book is a tad bit different from the traditional cycle touring book. When hearing that I was creating an Oregon Coast cycling guide, a medical doctor I know asked: "Is it going to be just the same old boring turn-to-turn mileage log with a few photos thrown in for good measure?" That motivated me.

Being a little odd and off in left field to begin with, the challenge to be different was something I relished. Right off the bat, there is one big difference between me and about 99.9% of all the rest of the cycle touring community, and certainly authors of books describing cycling routes. For one thing, I have never ridden a bicycle on the Oregon Coast! Nope, not even one city block. Bicycles aren't my thing. I find them uncomfortable for long rides, and to preserve my butt, I opt to be comfy when I am out here beholding the beauty of this beachy bounty. I'm weird.

Additionally, I live in Oregon, and everyone knows that Oregon is weird. Instead of a bike, I ride a recumbent rig called a tadpole tricycle, with two wheels up front, and one large drive wheel in the rear, a race trike with the capability to move its pilot along at lightning-fast white-knuckle speeds. So, while I've never ridden a bicycle the full length of the Oregon Coast, I have indeed pedaled a tricycle that distance, and I even kept going much farther south, all the way to Morro Bay, California.

This is the "bike" I ride, called a trike – a fast 'n fun machine!

I understand the world of long haul cycling pretty well, especially since I have lived smack dab in the middle of the route described in this book for over twenty years. Even when I'm not out there pedaling, I am watching you all go by, loaded with panniers and having a grand adventure in the sun and rain, and on the hills. I enjoy the show as an observer too. One of my favorite things to do is hang out at the bike shop and meet coastal bikers.

In reality, we are all out there doing the same exact thing: pedaling our living human bodies and cargo over incredibly long distances as measured by folks using human power, and we are expending about 5,000 or more calories each day while doing it. It's really tough work, regardless of our physical conditioning and experience because most of us have a tendency to ride at the level we are able to maintain. This coast is hard, but it's really worth it!

Yes, we are all cyclists, whether on two or three wheels, and we all share the joy and exhilaration of touring in really neat places. We seek the challenge, the camaraderie of fellow cyclists, and the realization that we moved ourselves from here to there using our own muscles rather than behemoth toxic automobiles. There is a certain sense of inner accomplishment that non-cyclists will never know. We use the same roads, yet in parallel universes.

HOW IS THIS BOOK DIFFERENT?

Back when I first decided to pedal from my central Oregon coast home down to Morro Bay in California, my cycling buddy Matt Jensen loaned me an excellent and popular book written by Tom Kirkendall and Vicky Spring, called *Bicycling the Pacific Coast*. It was a route guide from Canada to Mexico, and it provided sufficient details that I had a fair idea of what to expect on my pending 875 mile ride south. It was an old 1998 edition, with a few photos, nice maps, basic short descriptions of each section, and a detailed mileage log. What I found interesting was that the mileages were broken down into <u>tenths</u>. In other words, this was a route guide for folks focused on odometer precision. Needed?

While I'll also be talking about mileages in this book, my main focus in that regard will simply be a reference to milepost markers along Oregon Coast Highway 101, which begin at MP 1 over the mighty wide Columbia River on the notorious 4-mile long Astoria-Megler bridge, and end at MP 363 at the California border south of Brookings, Oregon. When I describe portions of the ride that branch off of Highway 101, these milepost markers will not be discussed, nor will I be giving the detailed mileages listed by tenths of a mile (absolutely unnecessary on this coast).

My intent is to focus primarily on the ambiance of it all, and significantly less on the precise mile to mile and turn by turn descriptions. On my overland trike, I do not have any electronic devices, so when I ride, my only mileage references are the milepost markers. It keeps my mind active. I don't keep an eye glued to an odometer, anticipating the next turn, missing the view.

In this bizarre book I also will be introducing you to some alternate routes that are not usually mentioned in cycling books, such as the secluded Otter Crest Loop south of Depoe Bay (awesome and really worth it), and the North Bend and Coos Bay work-around, which bypasses the huge bridge and the two busy towns completely for those who prefer it. It's an option for some.

Experience cycling with many other avid overland riders has shown me that most of us pedal these routes for the cycling itself, and rarely have I ever observed anyone opting to do all the traditional tourist oriented activities, such as lengthy hikes, or protracted off-route backroads that require yet more of our already well-worked bodies. When we reach our night's camp, our minds are focused on simply relaxing: pitching a tent, taking a shower, eating food, and hitting the sack! That's a cyclist's life!

The spectacular view from the top of the Otter Crest loop awaits cyclists, avoiding busy Highway 101 with no distant vistas.

Basically, in this book, I will endeavor to do much less with precise mileages (not needed on the Oregon Coast), and spend more time on chatting with you just as if we are cycling partners doing the ride together. One thing that makes this easier for me is that I'll just be taking about 383 miles from the Columbia River to the California border. This allows for more time to ponder interesting things along the way, including stuff like some ghosts of the Oregon Coast – find that in other cycling books! Town histories will also be a part of this ride – fun to know how these places got started! Detailed mile by mile talk, broken down into tenths, is simply not necessary on the Oregon Coast because of its straightforward nature. Let's just have fun!

Precise mileage information really shines when going through the huge metro areas, such as the crowded and urbanized Sausalito and San Francisco region, but such extreme detail isn't necessary on this bike route. Out here on this coast, there is not even one huge city with a maze of streets to navigate. Essentially, we simply follow Highway 101 nearly the whole way, and this is super easy to do even if you've never been here before. There are only a handful of spots where we will exit 101 for a more scenic alternate route, and I will verbally describe them to you, and show photographs of the turns. It's a snap – trust me!

Another really nice aspect of Oregon's portion of 101 is that, unlike California, there are no parts of it that turn into mega freeways, where all of a sudden you discover that bicyclists are not allowed to ride. It's all pretty darn rural feeling out here along Oregon's section, called the Oregon Coast Highway (OCH).

Regarding mileage, it's all so approximate in the reality of the ride anyway, because we all make different daily decisions out here that affect the number displayed on one's odometer. Why deal with technical stuff when so much beauty and excitement surround us? When taking this coastal route, becoming immersed in mileage calculations, or even worrying about all those very intimidating elevation profiles that are ultra compressed to the point that it seems you will be scaling Mount Everest, is just an added component for those who prefer it. My message in this book is that we can just pedal and have fun like in the good old days! All you truly need to ride the **Oregon Coast Bike Route** is a bike, cargo bags, water, and an exceptionally fit human body!

I also wish to spend more time discussing some tips for making a coastal ride more enjoyable, such as traveling very light and easy, preparing for raccoon incursions at night, and taking time to stop now and then to enjoy local flavor. The average time for a bike tourist to travel the Oregon Coast is 6-8 days, which is readily doable for a fit rider, but one could take, say, 10 days or more, and really see it much more intimately. Less fit riders will need more time. Do your own pace.

There is certainly no shortage of campgrounds, markets, bathrooms, or scenery, so this trip is made to order if you have gotten past the initial cycling fears of automobiles that many neophytes have. Most of the Oregon Coast Highway has really nice and wide shoulders, allowing for relaxed appreciation of the views, but when the road travels up around the capes and heads, the pavement narrows and shoulders disappear, causing the state to post huge yellow warning signs for motorists that we human powered humans are in the road with them!

Beware of private campgrounds with standard trash receptacles! Raccoons will keep you awake all night as they look for food.

Most cyclists travel from north to south, for two very good reasons: 1) By pedaling south, you are on the ocean side of the road for the best views and photographs, and 2) the prevailing winds during summer are out of the northwest, and tend to make your ride easier. If you pedal the other direction, from California to the Columbia River, many afternoons would find you battling powerful headwinds. Argh! That can get real old real fast, as I have learned over the years as I pedal the coastal regions for my personal day rides. You don't want to do this either. But it will make you strong! Thousands have already learned this lesson.

I will not be laying out each day's travel for you because I have no idea of your own goals or abilities. I will be presenting knowledge that will allow you do decide what best suits your own needs and schedule. With so many campgrounds along the way (16 state parks with camp facilities alone, not including other government and private campgrounds), it's really quite easy to figure a daily schedule that is just right for your unique trip. I'll discuss where key things are located, using milepost markers as indicators, and you'll be doing the actual implementation.

A WORD ABOUT THE MAPS

Maps are perhaps the most challenging thing to prepare for a book, as decisions must be made regarding how much of what kind of information to put on each image. Since books are small compared to a regular paper map that folds out into a large area, I've prepared a series of maps that each depicts a different series of objects, for simplicity. These are not your typical maps though.

Some of you may expect really detailed maps as found online, easily resizeable on computer screens, or maps similar to fold-out paper maps, which I like to use. I am not offering those maps in these pages. All of us can easily refer to them through other sources prior to the trip if we have detailed questions. This book aims to offer a new experience. I'm weird, and so are the maps I have put in these pages. Some may be useless, but they are at least entertaining and unique, as you shall discover shortly.

If you find these maps in this book useful, feel free to photocopy and laminate them to carry in your handlebar bag. Carrying an entire book is heavy, and not recommended, but once you have read it, the maps will likely get you exactly where you want to go, so just take them for reference. Or, if you are a light overland traveler, take the whole book to read at your tent site.

Tsunami waves do occur on this ride, once every few hundred years, but no cyclist has been wiped out yet! You might be the first. If you are in the zone when one comes, pedal like hell up a very steep road! This bar is at Wheeler, Oregon, on Nehalem Bay. Have fun while the ocean sleeps! Never ever turn your back!

THE SEVEN ADVENTURE MAPS:

Okay, I will now reveal my versions of maps, quite different from probably anything you've seen before, or will likely see again. This book aims to leave the normal behind in many ways, and this is one of the ways I will be expressing my alternative brain. Since this route is so darn straightforward, compared to parts of California cities that are a mind-boggling nightmare to navigate, fun oriented maps will serve the purpose well.

I am but a happy jester at heart, a sentient human creature with a very limited time in this form of existence, so laughing and doing that which is not commonly done are my calling cards, and since I create and write books to amuse my own head, it is of less concern to me what others think. I hope this stuff is useful to you, yet I'm not out to make a fortune directing bikers at the beach.

Map of Towns: Many coastal towns are shown on this map, although some unincorporated are not. No metropolitan cities exist on the Oregon coast, making navigation by cyclists easy and relaxing, with use of GPS devices totally unnecessary. Save the weight, and leave the GPS at home if only riding Oregon's coast.

Map of Counties: This map labels the counties found along the Oregon coastline, along with the milepost markers (MP) where the county lines are found. The county lines are signed well.

Map of Mileposts: To further help orient you along the way, this map shows approximate locations of main milepost markers, starting at MP 1 and ending with MP 363. Our route will be closer to 383 miles though, counting the bicycling side loops.

Map of Oregon State Park Campgrounds: This map shows the locations of the sixteen coastal state parks that are ideal for cyclists. Well spaced and incredibly scenic, these state parks offer hiker/biker camps for $6.00 currently, and you get a hot shower every night to boot! They are my favorites. Other campgrounds will also be discussed within this book, such as Forest Service.

Map of Lighthouses: The Oregon Coast has 11 lighthouses to warn seafaring ships away from the dangerous rocks. This map shows all eleven of the coastal Oregon lighthouses. Two are privately owned. Many of them you can actually tour inside!

Map of Steep Hilly Intense Terrain: This map shows where you will encounter some really steep portions of the coastal ride. Also on this map are significant bridges and the two tunnels you will have to survive – cars are required to limit speed to 30 MPH when cyclists are in the tunnels. They are well lit inside, and motorists can easily see you. Don't stress over them – ride easy!

Map of Ghost Stories: The Oregon Coast is home to a few fabled ghost tales, some of which will be discussed in this book, so this map will show where the ghosts are found. Camp in ghost-free zones! The only ghost I've seen is the Oregon Coast Cycling Ghost, whom I shall introduce later in this book.

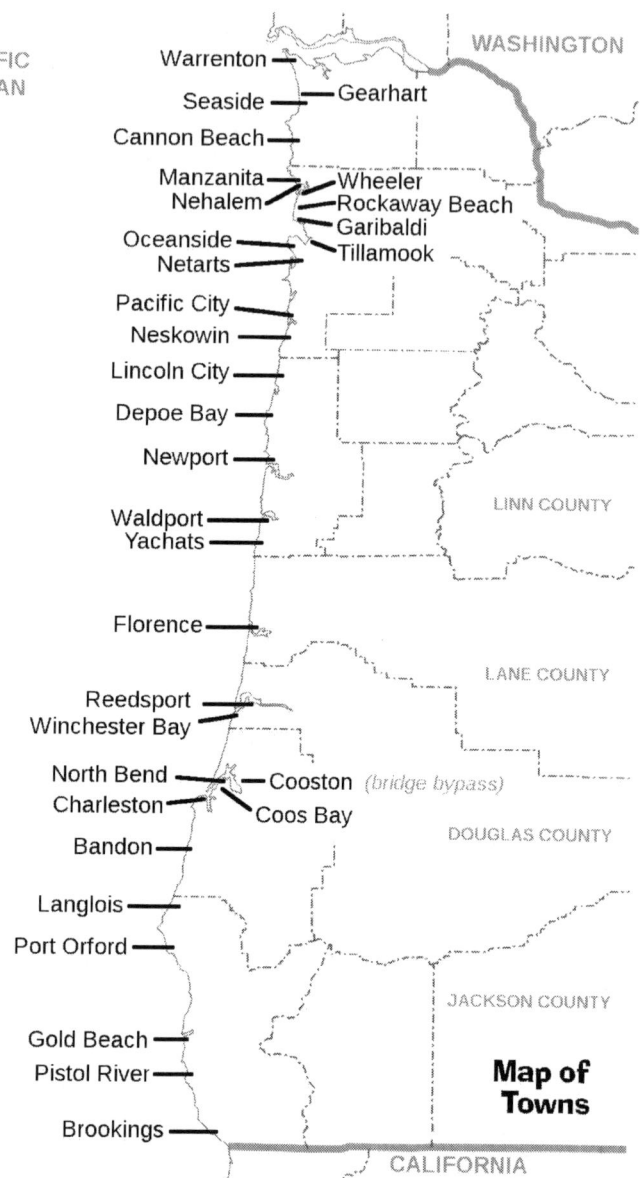

Map of Towns

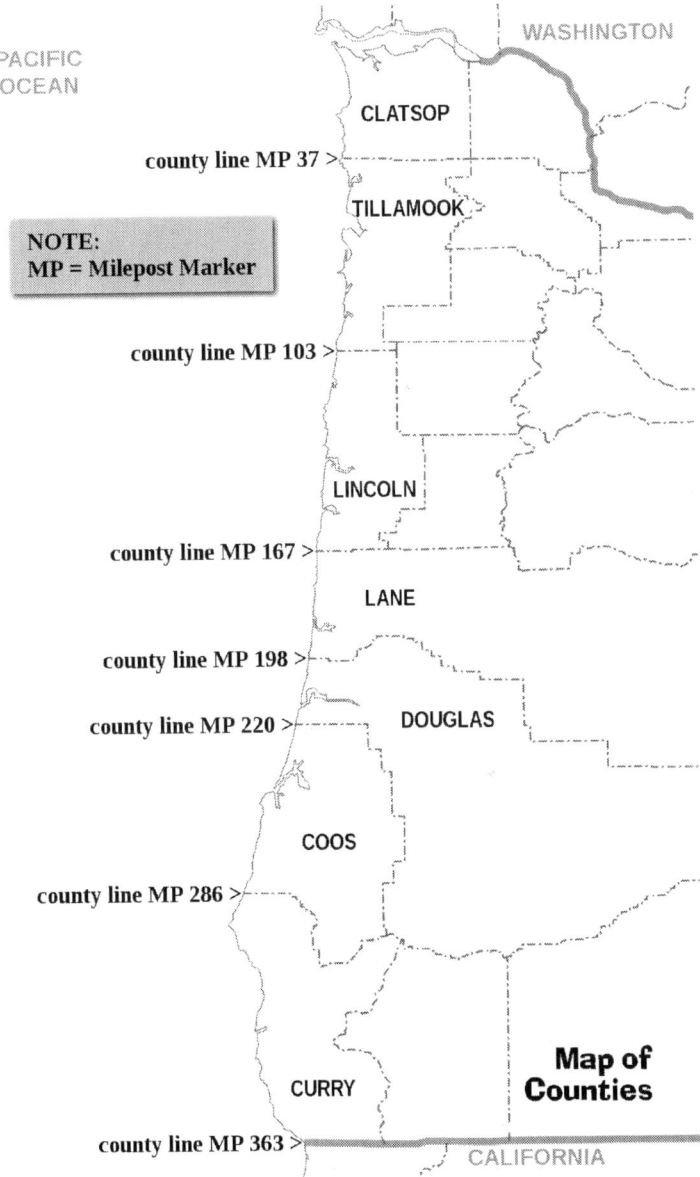

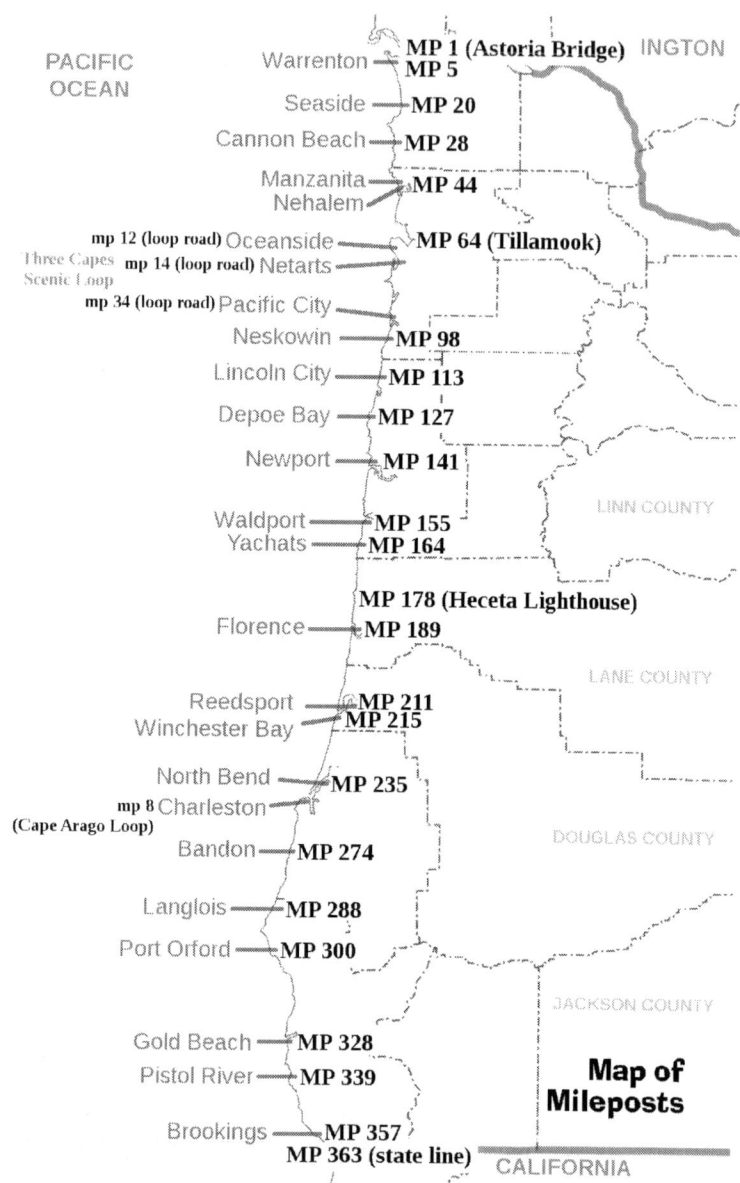

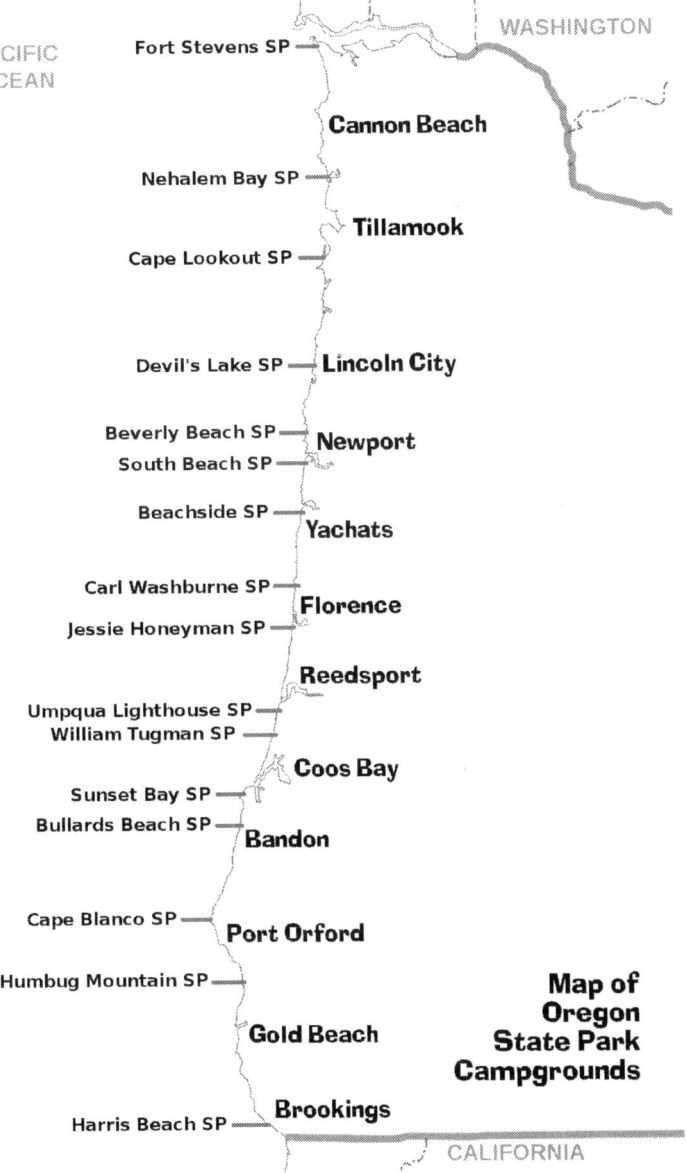

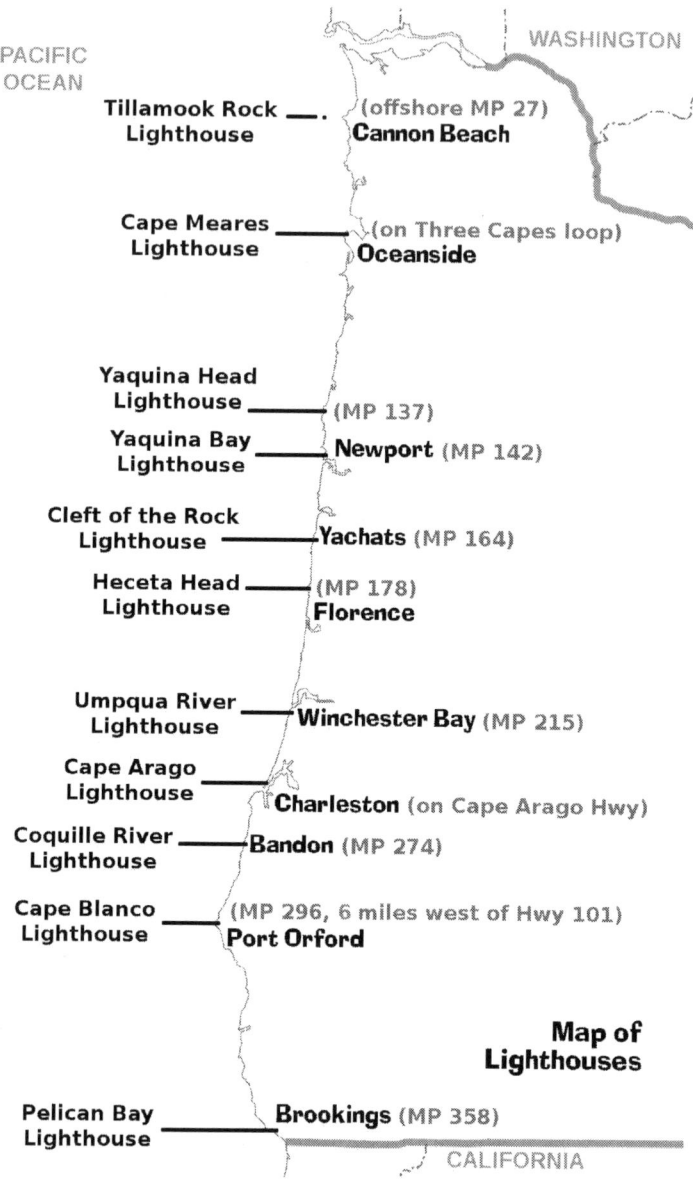

Map of Lighthouses

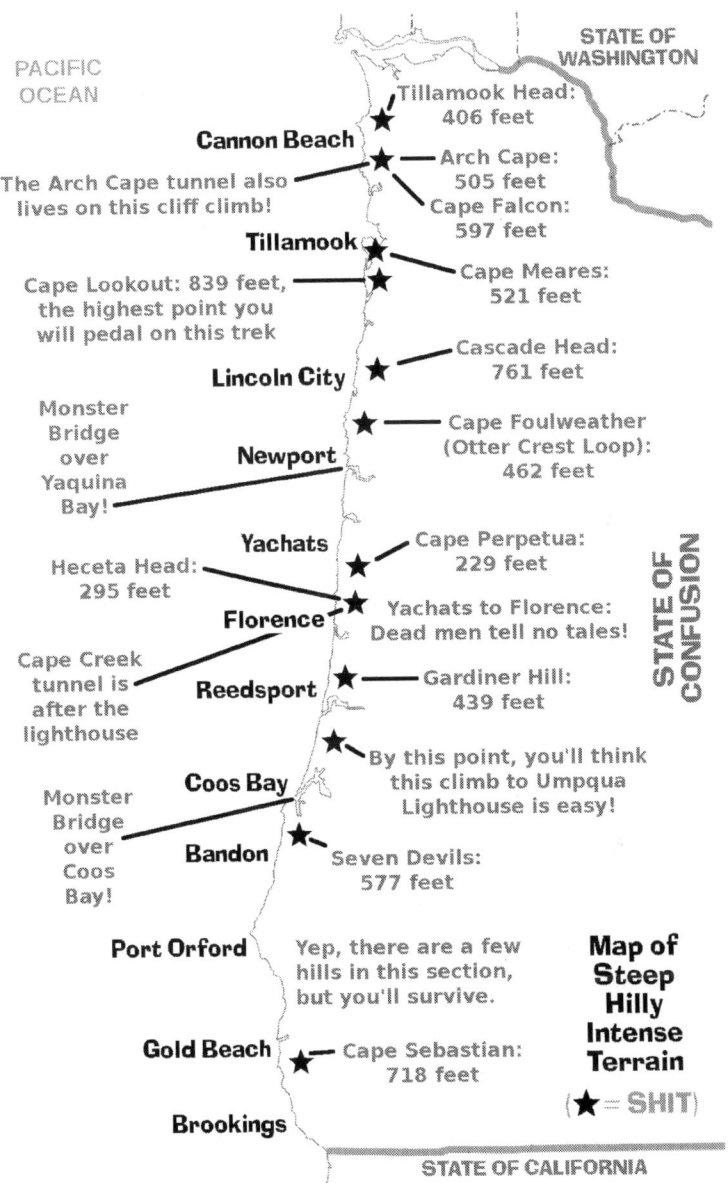

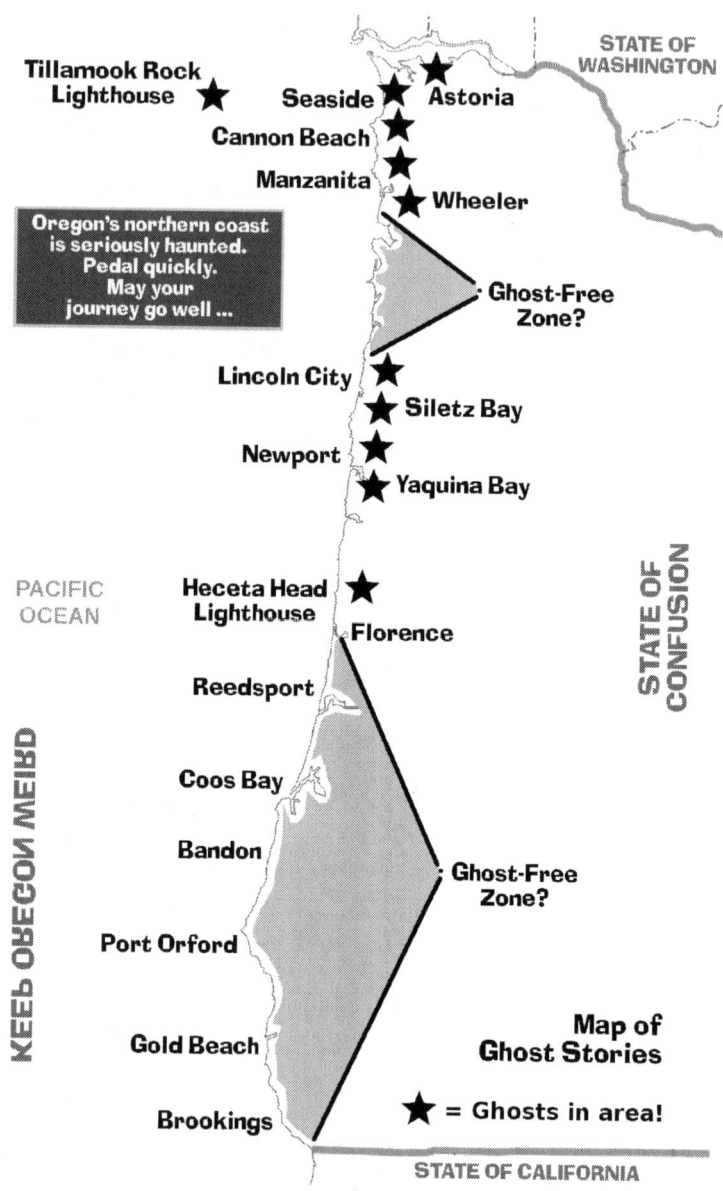

Steep Hilly Intense Terrain

It is a very common notion that since this cycling route lies along the coast of the Pacific Ocean, it must therefore be relatively flat, and thus a fairly easy ride compared to when a cyclist pedals over mountain ranges like the Coast Range, Cascade Range, or Sierra Nevada Range. I have heard this thought expressed by several pedal pushers who had not yet attempted the **Oregon Coast Bike Route**, and, somewhat embarrassingly enough, my own head originally suggested this ease before I rode it for the first time.

After all, I had pedaled my human powered trike to Death Valley and southern California, and there were many long and daunting stretches over huge mountains that presented themselves in my path. The coast, by comparison, had to be much easier. After my first time of doing it though, I learned the reality of the road here on the coast. Everyone who rides it does!

Yes indeed, there certainly is quite a bit of S̲teep H̲illy I̲ntense T̲errain on this 383 mile ride, or what some cyclists who live in these parts enjoy referring to in the form of an acronym, meaning the initials of the first letter of each word. For them, this ride is full of SHIT (Steep Hilly Intense Terrain).

Keep in mind that my intent here is merely to inform you, among other things, about the local flavor of the weird coast of Oregon and the people who inhabit the region. My personal values of common decency and appropriate writing behavior prohibit usage of potentially inappropriate material, yet I simply wish to share the regional ambiance of the cycling cult.

When riding this spectacular route, you will frequently be presented with blue and white road signs that remind you of the dangers you face should there be a big earthquake off in the ocean somewhere. As you pedal down into low lying places, of which there are many on the coast, you will be greeted with the news that you are entering a tsunami zone. The graphic shows a hapless human about to be engulfed by a monstrous ocean wave, as he futilely runs towards higher ground to save his pathetic little self. Running is slow however, so the good news is that you are pedaling a bike or a trike, and can get to that higher ground in time to watch the Pacific Ocean consume the Oregon Coast, and all those unlucky folks who are running and screaming far below.

Then, a bit farther south of this sign, you'll eventually notice yet another blue and white sign, but this one has good news, from a tsunami standpoint that is, but bad news from a cycling standpoint. The good news is that you are leaving the tsunami hazard zone, but the bad news is that this means you will be pedaling up some hills for a while, sometimes up some very steep and long hills, such as on the capes and heads, known as headlands, of this coastline. Of course, uphills make us stronger! Riding through SHIT however has a positive effect on one's healthy lifespan. Cyclists DO live longer than normal people!

Many of the coastal towns here are found in tsunami hazard zones, or what I like to call sandlands, the low spots of the coast. An excellent example of one such town is a place where they specialize in making cheese, a famous spot called Tillamook.

In reality, no part of this ride reaches the lowness of sea level. It is always a little bit above that line, most of the time. When tsunamis hit, many parts of the **Oregon Coast Bike Route**

are below sea level, at least for a time, as the surging ocean buries the land, recedes, and then buries it again with each successive shock wave of water. If you happen to be the cyclist lucky enough to actually experience a tsunami while riding this awesome route, do two things please: 1) Send me an email with the story and photos, and 2) pedal to high ground and camp up there for at least one night to be sure it's over. The route forward though may be blocked the next week by fallen trees, wrecked homes, and ruined cars. Be careful not to get back on the road too quickly!

The LEAVING TSUNAMI HAZARD ZONE sign means you will be climbing again ... to safety! A big tsunami devastates the coast roughly every 300-600 years. It has currently been around 300 years. Statistically, you have decided to ride within this time frame. Better watch your GPS for escape routes!

This cycling route may indeed be full of SHIT, however this brings up one of the thrills associated with the varied terrain. That is, for every seriously intense climb up the side of a coastal cape or head, there is an equally serious descent on the other side! What goes up, must come down. This we know because why? Well, because we begin this journey essentially at sea level (jetty at Fort Stevens State Park on the Columbia River) and we end the journey at a slightly higher elevation, at the California state line, south of Harris Beach State Park. Low to low. But not flat. There are about **16,000** feet (**4900** meters) of elevation rise and fall on this journey. That which does not kill us makes us stronger! Argh

So, if we end essentially where we began elevation wise, then for each of these monster killer uphills, we know very well that we'll be going back down. And what a ride those down sections are! Do you like traveling along between 40 to 50 miles per hour on your bicycle loaded with cargo? This is where I am very content to be riding my tricycle, a low slung rocket ship with three wheels that feels like a Lamborghini sports car coming down. My rear end is only seven inches above the pavement, less distance to fall in a crash. Feels like a go-cart! What about you?

All this talk about Steep Hilly Intense Terrain though is not to minimize the flat sections of the **Oregon Coast Bike Route**, of which there are many along the way. You will be pedaling for mile after mile along nearly flat roadway, most of which is pretty well paved for smooth riding enjoyment. You will like these stretches after all the SHIT you've been through, although you may even question the flats as you lose the fillings in your teeth through the Rockaway Beach region south of Nehalem Bay State Park, as this chip sealed roadbed is about the **most unpleasant** of the entire trip to the California state line.

And once you do reach the California line, you can visibly see, and noticeably feel, the difference in paving compared to Oregon – right at the line, it is clear the flat road changes dramatically. Perhaps the state to the south was so extravagant on its paving that the expenditures were part of the reason for its subsequent bankruptcy. Oh well, Oregon is not in much better financial condition from what I hear, so it is incumbent upon all us touring cyclists to get out there and help pump up the ailing economies. The good news is that by doing so, we are extending our life through healthy exercise while really enjoying all that the natural world has to offer. It's win/win.

From Manzanita to Tillamook, the road is either downhill or flat, as seen in the photo above, however this particular portion through the Rockaway Beach area is miserable pavement to ride. Notice this rare pedestrian covered bridge. Things such as this are not seen elsewhere. The road hurts too much to enjoy it though.

FIVE FLYING SAUCERS AT THE BEACH

When you pedal through towns on the **Oregon Coast Bike Route**, you will see these tall weird looking devices if you are observant. These are tsunami siren towers, and the state of Oregon has them in areas where people live in inundation zones because sometimes things get deadly wet! These sirens are loud!

TSUNAMI FACTS
(courtesy State of Oregon)

The earthquakes that cause tsunamis in Oregon can occur nearby or in distant areas like Alaska or Russia. A severe earthquake associated with the Cascadia Subduction Zone off the Oregon coast would generate a destructive tsunami impacting coastal communities within minutes. A locally generated tsunami has the potential to cause damage that far exceeds the damage inflicted by a tsunami of distant origin.

Tsunamis generated in distant locations of the Pacific Basin can take four hours or longer to reach Oregon's coastline. In the deepest ocean waters a tsunami is unrecognizable and can travel over 500 miles per hour. As the tsunami approaches the coastline, and shallower water, its speed slows and wave height increases dramatically. But, the tsunami still moves faster than a person can run once it reaches the shoreline. Sometimes, the tsunami's arrival is preceded by a noticeable withdrawal of the water. The configuration of the near-shore ocean bottom and coastline play tricks with the tsunami waves. They can cause the waves to amplify in one area and be weakened in another nearby area. Tsunamis are unpredictable as they come ashore and flood low-lying areas. Harbors, bays and river mouths are very sensitive to tsunamis. Unpredictable currents, terrifying waves, and water level oscillations that can last for hours will play havoc with ships, boats, and dock facilities. (*hey, what about bicycles?*)

The rapidly increasing sea level caused by the tsunami picks up debris, rocks, logs and other materials that act as projectiles that further destroy buildings and cause casualties. Sand deposited by a prehistoric tsunami that occurred around the year 1700 caused destructive, flooding waves that impacted much of the Oregon coastline. This tsunami was preceded by a severe earthquake, magnitude 8 or possibly greater, that caused land along the coast to sink before it was inundated by the huge tsunami waves. Historic records from Japan tie the arrival of unusual waves along the Japan coastline to this earthquake and tsunami generated off the Oregon coast!

On March 28, 1964, a tsunami hit the Oregon coastline about four hours after it was generated by a severe earthquake in

Prince William Sound, Alaska. Four people in Oregon were killed by this tsunami. Destruction occurred at numerous locations, including Seaside, Cannon Beach, Depoe Bay, Florence, Rogue River, along the Umpqua River, Waldport and in Newport Bay.

THE COAST IS CLEAR ... SOMETIMES

Weather here on the coast can be fickle. I have found the ideal time for riding to be the month of September. Most of the traffic is gone by then, especially after Labor Day, because all the families with kids have departed. Usually what's left is the retired crowd that drives the mobile homes, and, of course, the locals. This month typically has mild temperatures, perfect for cycling up the long capes and heads, and days are still long enough to provide time to find a camp or motel. September generally has the least chance of precipitation, so it's a good bet!

By April of the year, rain often is beginning to lessen, but I have seen notable exceptions, with heavy rains continuing into May and even June. Living on the central coast, I get to see when the first cyclists begin coming through each year on OCH 101, and I have witnessed riders getting drenched in June. Of course, this is not always the case, and even during wetter years, May and June can have many sunny and wonderful cycling days. It's pretty much a situation where it's the luck of the draw. Roll the dice!

By July, chances of dry and warmer weather dramatically increase, even in wetter years, and by the time August comes to this coastal wonderland, days are warm and usually sunny. I have found my best riding here to be September. Can it rain then? Yes, it can, and sometimes does, but again, it's all a matter of chance. We have the time allotted for the Oregon Coast trip, and basically we take what we get. Often we get lucky. Sometimes we don't. Other times, there is ideal weather with an occasional day of the wet stuff just to keep us on our toes. There are NO guarantees!

October is getting rather late, and rains are again starting to enshroud the Oregon Coast region. Temperatures are also on the decline, with daytime highs in the lower 50s. But, then again, there are awesome sunny days in October too. If you want to play it safe, and you have options, opt for July, August, or September.

Regardless of when you ride the Legend, carry rain gear in your panniers! It is quite possible you will not need it, but then again, better safe than sorry. Mornings are usually cool, and fog is always a possible item on the menu each day, even in afternoons! If an afternoon fog conspires with wind, it WILL get very nippy.

GETTING HERE AND BACK HOME AGAIN

I have become spoiled during the two decades of living on the Oregon Coast! Being in the midst of the **Oregon Coast Bike Route**, I can ride any or all of it at my whim. I don't even own a car! What about all the other riders who have to get over to the western coast of the United States to simply begin the trip? Cyclists flock by the thousands to the Oregon Coast with their bicycles from all over the planet. What do they do?

Okay, the big thing you'll want to know comes out of the place where we do not even start this coastal ride south, and that is Astoria! For all you fellow cyclists who must do the dreaded petroleum transit solution, the Astoria-Warrenton Visitor Center has your problem solved! Here is the hot scoop:

If you drive yourself and your bike to the visitor center, you will be allowed to park your car there for the duration of the ride down the Oregon Coast, or even all the way to San Francisco for that matter. All summer long, cyclists are allowed to park their cars in the back parking lot. You simply fill out their registration form, put their special pass on your car's dashboard, and take off pedaling for the California state line! There is really no set time limit either – just tell 'em where you're going, when you expect to be back, give your contact info, and you're all set. If you fail to return in a reasonable time frame, they will follow up to find out if you need assistance by calling you on your cell phone.

Well, that sounds great, but how do I get back to Astoria once down in San Francisco or Brookings? Nancy at the visitor center informs me that many cyclists who ride to San Francisco just catch a Greyhound bus back up to Portland, and then once there, two buses run to Astoria daily, where you will be reunited with your automobile. If you end in Brookings, have your bike boxed at Escape Hatch Sports, send it wherever you wish, and get public transportation home (see bike shop listing at end of book).

Astoria-Warrenton Visitor Center
111 West Marine Drive (P.O. Box 176)
Astoria, Oregon 97103-0176
travelastoria.com/about/visitor-center.html
visitors@oldoregon.com / 1-800-875-6807

MILEAGES BETWEEN PLACES

Oregon Coast Bike Route (*mileages are approximate*)

Clatsop Spit to Seaside:	20 miles
Seaside to Cannon Beach:	08 miles
Cannon Beach to Nehalem:	17 miles
Nehalem to Rockaway Beach:	07 miles
Rockaway Beach to Tillamook:	13 miles
Tillamook to Pacific City:	33 miles (via 3 Capes)
Pacific City to Lincoln City:	25 miles
Lincoln City to Depoe Bay:	14 miles
Depoe Bay to Newport:	14 miles (via Otter)
Newport to Waldport:	15 miles
Waldport to Yachats:	09 miles
Yachats to Florence:	26 miles
Florence to Reedsport:	21 miles
Reedsport to North Bend:	24 miles
North Bend to Bandon:	36 miles (via 7 Devils)
Bandon to Langlois:	14 miles
Langlois to Port Orford:	12 miles
Cape Blanco (out & back)	12 miles
Port Orford to Gold Beach:	28 miles
Gold Beach to Pistol River:	11 miles
Pistol River to Brookings:	18 miles
Brookings to California:	06 miles
Clatsop Spit to California:	383 miles (via bike rte.)

NOTE: This route is not complicated, and it does not go through any metro areas that require point to point mileage figures. Avoid the initial temptation to get overly concerned about mileages – <u>Don't</u> get hung-up on these numbers! The road signing is quite excellent, and it's easy to find the way. Towns can be up to 5 miles long, so distances from town to town will vary depending on where the calculation began (center of town to center of next town, or leading edge?) When I first enter a town, I consider myself having arrived. It's best to simply enjoy the ride, and let mileage concerns fade away! Love the view! Ride the Legend!

WE BEGIN OUR JOURNEY ON THE BEACH

I mentioned a few pages ago that I was not going to present you an itinerary of each day, or suggest how far you should ride, or where you should camp. This is because I do not know what you are capable of, or what your own ideas of daily mileages might be. You may be riding supported by a vehicle, with no cargo on your rig, so daily mileages might be quite high, compared to folks who carry 30 pounds of gear.

I will however make a statement about the start of this journey through Oregon. The beginning of my presentation in this book does not occur on the Oregon Coast Highway (OCH) 101. This is because I am suggesting commencement of this trek up at Oregon's most extreme northwestern point, a small bit of sandy beach area that juts out into the Columbia River, which separates the states of Oregon and Washington. More on this a little later.

Here is where we begin, on a sandy beach too deep to pedal. You must carry your bike or trike out here! The mountains to the left are in Washington, those to the right in Oregon. The 4 mile wide Columbia River separates the two states. The ocean is behind me.

The Oregon Coast is simple to navigate via cycle power. Everything is very well signed along the way, and, unlike high speed automobiles, where a turn could be easily missed in some situations, pedaling this rural coastline on a bike is slow enough that you have plenty of time to read the signs and get it right!

CRAZY GUY ON A BIKE JOURNAL

Most every cyclist on Planet Earth today who takes a long trip on a human powered bicycle or tricycle documents the journey online, at the **Crazy Guy On A Bike** website. This resource is a place where normal people like you and me (well, perhaps not me) can post their stories and photos of their most excellent cycling adventure. It will motivate you! Over 100,000 daily hits!

Once you complete your Oregon Coast cycling odyssey, be sure to write the day by day story, just as it unfolded in all its glory and guts, and share it with the world. Thousands of cyclists all over the planet read this website, and you too can become a cycling hero to the masses of folks who are either about to travel the same route you did, or simply like to live vicariously through the wild adventures of others who actually did take the trips. You can post your stuff on **CGOAB** at no charge, including all your photographs. Of course, publisher Neil Gunton has expenses in doing this for us all, thus if you feel so inclined, you can also make a donation to the cause. Visit: **crazyguyonabike.com**

There is one thing however that I must caution you about if you are going to post your ride to **CGOAB**. There is no "R" in Bandon! Okay, now to sign off from this short chapter, I'll use the laid-back cyclist jargon favored by Neil: "**Hasta la Pasta**."

WHAT'S UP WITH ASTORIA?

Why isn't Astoria listed on all the maps in this book? Why is it only on the ghost map? Doesn't the **Oregon Coast Bike Route** go through Astoria? Has it been overlooked? Nope! Here's why:

The northwestern most point is where we start, on a sandy beach!

Okay, here's the scoop, direct from my human powered brain: I wanted to begin this ride at the northwestern-most point in the State of Oregon. Welch Island is farther to the north, on the Columbia River, and Cape Blanco is farther to the west, down by

Port Orford, but there is only <u>one</u> place that is the farthest north AND west in the state, and that is the little slice of sandy land where you saw my trike parked on the beach.

It goes by a couple of names: Columbia River South Jetty, and also the Clatsop Spit. Well, I suppose some could call it other names too, especially those drivers who stick their cars in the deep sand while attempting to drive to the water, but that's irrelevant. I carried my trike out for the photograph for three reasons: 1) trikes don't do well in sand, 2) I didn't want to get sand in the drivetrain, 3) there was a pickup truck stuck up to its axles in my way. You can't pedal the entire trip, but you can walk.

There is a bike path much the way from the hiker/biker camp at Fort Stevens State Park to the northwestern most point in Oregon, located on the Columbia River South Jetty. This is heading north.

Now, if you are familiar with the route of the Adventure Cycling Association, you probably realize that their ride does not hit the Pacific Coast until the State of Oregon, as it comes from inland Washington. For the record, the coastal route through Washington is also a great cycling ride, but much of it is also inland. It is the Oregon Coast that really gets down to business with the views and water! Few ride the Washington coast.

If you are doing this coastal route using Highway 101 from Washington, you will be crossing the huge Astoria-Megler bridge over the Columbia River, just a ways east of the ocean. This bridge is a tad over 4 miles long, and is only for cars and cyclists – no pedestrians are allowed. The first two thirds of the bridge is low and flat, but the final section on the Oregon side rises spookily high in the air, over the river channel.

So, if you are coming from the north, and you wish to begin the Oregon adventure as recommended in this book, once you get off the Astoria bridge, hang a right, cross Youngs Bay, and then follow the signs to Fort Stevens State Park. This is where you will spend your first night of this trip. Do it right!

Oh yeah, even though we don't start our cycling odyssey in Astoria, the first **ghost** of this journey is found there! His name is Paul, and he dresses in a Panama hat and a white tuxedo. If you can locate the historic Liberty Theater, a vaudeville palace established in the 1920s, you'll find Paul. He is blamed for weird things like stuff flying through the air, bizarre noises, and slamming doors. And yes, he does have some friends, in case you happen to miss him. Paul's **airy buddies** must have been firemen, because they inhabit the realm of the Astoria Firehouse.

The original inhabitants of this region were the Clatsop people. Captain Robert Gray sailed into the Columbia River in 1792. Later, the Lewis and Clark Corps of Discovery expedition spent a winter at Fort Clatsop in 1805. Astoria is the oldest American settlement west of the Rocky Mountains, getting its start when John Astor created his fur trading post in 1811. In 1912, John's great grandson went down with the Titanic. Oh, and Arnold's movie, *Kindergarten Cop*, was also filmed here. Wow!

FORT STEVENS STATE PARK

The journey I am describing in this book begins at Fort Stevens State Park, which covers 4,247 acres of wooded coastal territory. More than 220,000 people from all over the world camp here every year. The original earthen fort was built in 1865 to protect the mouth of the Columbia River from confederate gun boats and

British ships during the American civil war. Fear built the fort!

The name of this state park originates from Isaac Stevens, a Washington territorial governor and a Union army general. He was terminated in 1862 at a battle zone. Oregon also used the fort during the Spanish-American war, world war one, and world war two, always to protect the Columbia. In June 1942, a Japanese submarine fired upon the fort. America was indeed attacked here!

A portion of the fort is shown here. You will enjoy pedaling the grounds, learning the history, and seeking out ghosts.

The method used by Japanese commander Tagami Meiji to enter these waters in his sub was to stealthily follow fishing boats, avoiding the mine fields. Late at night, the sub rose to the surface of the Columbia River, and fired a total of 17 rounds into the fort area. American war planes spotted the enemy submarine and began dropping bombs on it, but the commander was skilled enough to avoid being hit, and then submerged his vessel and escaped. No one was killed in all this shooting and bombing, but this spooked everyone, and barbed wire was then strung up and down the coastline here to keep out any future invaders.

This is a cool place to start with all its history. Besides the fort, a British chap named Peter Iredale, who owned a boat company in Liverpool, ordered his boat, named after him, to make a stop in Portland with 1,000 tons of cargo. Well, the night was very stormy, and the Peter Iredale ran up onto the beach in the high winds. That was in 1906, but you can still see the ship today by pedaling a short bike path from the hiker/biker camp to the beach. They were unsuccessful at refloating Peter's boat.

The Ft. Stevens hiker/biker camp is very large, flat, and wooded.

WARRENTON, OREGON

Fort Stevens State Park officially lies in Warrenton, Oregon, but this could be confusing because some older maps show the area as Warrenton-Hammond. Hammond used to be an incorporated town, but in 1991, the citizens voted to join up with their neighbor to the south, thus the city of Warrenton now includes Hammond. This area has a very rural country feeling to it.

Warrenton was platted in 1889, with the Pacific Ocean bordering the west side, and the Columbia River on the north side. It was named for Daniel Warren, one of its first settlers. Clara Munson was the first mayor here, and also the first female mayor in Oregon. Since Warrenton lies on tidal flats, dikes built by Chinese workers kept the river from flooding the town. So far the water has been kept out where it belongs, so you can camp!

WILD BUSHWHACKERS FOUND THE WAY

A little while ago, geologically speaking, a couple of guys seeking some high adventure began using a boat and their boots to paddle and hike out to this very northwestern area of what is now called Oregon. In 1804, these two chaps, along with a small motley crew of rugged adventurers, were sent westward from St. Charles, Missouri to map the new Louisiana Purchase, and lay claim to the wild western parts of the wilderness before England, France, or Spain could do so. America wanted to be first.

They were sent by a plantation slave holder to find the most expedient and direct water route to the west coast, right where Warrenton now sits. Their boss man also happened to be the third president of the United States, a man known as Thomas Jefferson. Their names were Meriwether Lewis and William Clark, and their epic walk and boat ride was called the Lewis and Clark Corps of Discovery. They make our ride seem like a snap!

Once they reached the Pacific Ocean, having paddled west down the Columbia River (no dams back then), they spent that winter at Fort Clatsop, not far from the hiker/biker camp at Fort Stevens State Park. It was a rainy miserable time for this tough team of bushwhackers, but they finally walked and paddled back home by 1806, with only one man losing his life along the way (due to illness). Many fascinating books have been written documenting their daunting trek out here.

This replica of their original winter fort is only a short diversion from the cycling route, and worth your time to visit. It is part of the Lewis and Clark National Historic Park. The fort is not far from the Oregon Coast Highway 101, and businesses where you can pick up supplies.

THE STATE OF OREGONIA

Perhaps a word about Oregon might be in order now that we are finally starting the 383 mile ride from Washington to California. Of course, I expect that since you are reading this book, you already have a pretty good idea of where Oregon lives, but might as well get it on record. This place is crazy, but fun.
    This state, one of 50 others in this country, is the ninth largest, being about 400 miles wide (west to east), and 360 miles long (north to south). Oregon is 98,381 square miles in area: the western region being wet, the central being quite mountainous, and the eastern being very desert-like in its terrain. We call them the wet side and dry side. The highest point is Mt. Hood (11,249 feet elevation), and the lowest is where we are pedaling. Portland

has the largest number of breweries on Plane Earth! Okay, that's quite a distinction. Portland is weird, and very proud of it too.

Former California state governor Arnold Schwarzenegger starred in a movie called *Kindergarten Cop*. It was filmed in Astoria, Oregon. Other movies filmed here include *One Flew Over the Cuckoo's Nest, Animal House,* and *The Goonies*. Portland, the weirdest place in the weirdest state, is also the hometown of Matt Groening, the guy who once started a irreverent animated show called *The Simpsons*. And if that's not enough to prove how wEirD we are here, a totally bizarre TV series called *Portlandia* features the city that seriously loves its beer. I strongly caution you about watching *Portlandia* on DVD.

In 1964, a company called Blue Ribbon Sports was founded in Beaverton, Oregon. A 1971 name change was based on the Greek goddess of victory, who, along with her siblings, were buddies of Zeus, who was the father of gods and men. This Greek goddess had the name of Nike, and now this famous running shoe company carries her name. If you like delicious fresh fruits, then you know about Harry & David, a couple of old farmers out Medford way who successfully founded a company of the same name in 1910. Now they ship pears all over the place, from online stores. With 8,000 employees, they are keeping Oregonians on the payroll and off the streets. Visit their main store in Medford if you can. Bring lots of cash though.

More good news is that residents of Oregon pay no sales tax on anything! Buy a car in California, and you pay the government three grand in taxes, but buy a car in Oregon, and you pay the government nothing! Whatever the price says in the store, that is precisely what you pay, to the cent. This is great news for Oregon Coast cyclists, because if the price indicates $5.95 in the market, you don't have to figure how much over six dollars it will be with tax. You'll get a nickel back in change.

Almost four million people live here in Oregon, and some of them don't want Californians moving up here. Even the former Californians who do live here adopt this mindset to keep any new Californians from moving behind them. It has been suggested that a wall be built at the state line to keep Oregon free of Californians, but that isn't really at all necessary. Why is this? Well, because some other people in this state started a big rumor years ago that it always rains here, and that seems to have done the trick. Californians just visit for a while, then return to their hot smog infested cities to earn money to pay for their mansions. Oregonians are more than happy to take Californians' money, just as long as the trespassers go back home after the purchase! Bikers are welcomed to move here though, because we love weirdos.

WHY OREGON COAST BUSINESS LOVES YOU

There are estimated between **8,000-10,000** cyclists pedaling the Oregon Coast every single summer season, swarming down (and sometimes up) the coast like cockroaches. Most of them ride bicycles, but a few really weird ones like me ride tricycles. We all are organic engines, using muscles. We produce no smog.

It's easy to spot a coastal touring cyclist! Their cycles are covered with an assortment of weather-worn bags, and a fair amount of road grime and grunge is visible, not only on the bike or trike, but also on the rider if (s)he has been on the road for more than a day or so. Frequently, they ride in pairs, often one large dirty male biker leading a smaller, but equally worn and stinky, female biker, but this is not always the case.

Many times over the years I have watched two lady bikers riding as a team, and every now and then, even a solo lady biker hauls on by. This is becoming more common, but the majority of solo riders are still the male ones. There are also larger groups of riders, usually associated with some outfit like Adventure Cycling Association, and some of the groups are not adorned with bags, which are being carried in the ACA support van. This is very expensive however! But it's fun nevertheless.

Well anyway, no matter how the riders come pedaling along here on the Oregon Coast, and no matter what they happen to be riding, Oregon businesses benefit because all cyclists spend lots of money every year, primarily on things like groceries, laundries, campgrounds, motels, and restaurants. So, when you spot a local cyclist friendly establishment, be sure to thank them for their efforts, and if they have something you need, give 'em your hard earned dollars, yen, pounds or whatever.

The Adventure Cycling Association van above is parked on a turnout at Arch Cape, as the paying clientèle pedal by up to the summit of Neahkahnie Mountain. This guy loves his job!

Above: rural market in Langlois, southern coast.
Below: beach motel in Pacific City, northern coast.

A cyclist pays for a hiker/biker campsite at Harris Beach State Park, Brookings, Oregon. Sites are now $6 nightly. Harris Beach, shown here, even has a laundry facility in the campground! Wow.

The only market in Garibaldi, Oregon, on the northern coast, is very well stocked, in case you can't wait the next 10 miles to Tillamook and its huge cheese factory. It's the first place in town.

SPIT FIRST, OR IT DOESN'T COUNT!

Based on a superficial in-depth review of all the written material about cycling the Oregon Coast, it has been determined that none, if not most, of the accounts don't get it right! They get it wrong!

This is the first-ever book that will reveal the **secret** to riding the **entire** Oregon Coast route, which, as you may have already gathered on previous pages, clearly does not begin on the Astoria-Megler bridge, or even Highway 101. To do this ride right, you must begin where it really counts: **SPIT FIRST**!

Riding the entire Oregon Coast means you begin at the Clatsop Spit, the **true point** of origination, another 5 miles north of the Fort Stevens campground. It's the one and **only way** to get the prized feather of this coastal route in your cap. The bike path begins just yards southwest of the hiker/biker camp. Ride due west to see the Peter Iredale shipwreck, then backtrack a ways to catch the path north to the spit, which ends a few miles up, with rough road taking you the rest of the way to the water's edge. Now, you have truly begun the **entire** coastal route to California!

This road heading south from the spit is rough, so ride slowly.

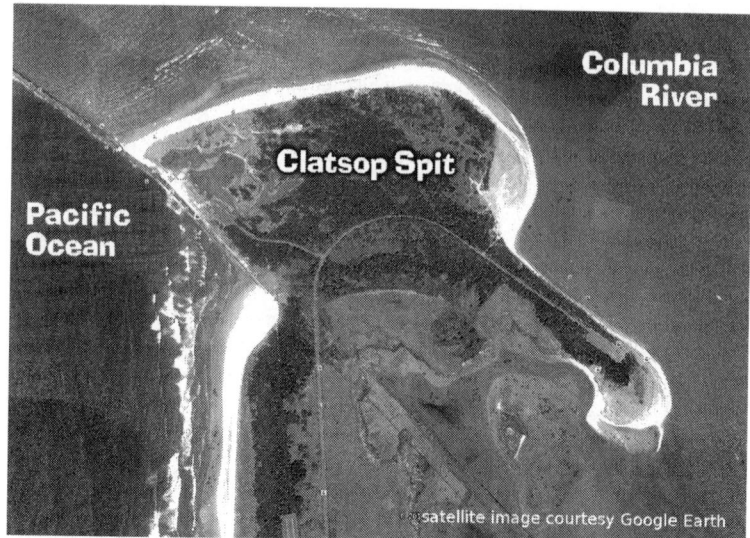

A satellite view of Clatsop Spit reveals its unique location. There are three places to access the beach and water here. Visit 'em all.

A hearty granola breakfast at Fort Stevens begins Day Two.

FORT STEVENS TO CANNON BEACH

Unlike other coastal cycling guidebooks, there will be no detailed listing of precise mileage beginning at zero for each section discussed in this book. You will discover that this route is simple and straightforward. From the hiker/biker camp, we just pedal out to the main entrance, turn right onto NW Ridge Road, and pedal south, following signs to Seaside. No matter if you take a slight wrong turn (hard to do), you'll hit the coast highway because it comes in at an angle from the east, intersecting our path of travel, not far south of Youngs Bay, shortly prior to MP 10 on Highway 101. Keep heading south and you'll run into 101, period.

    I suppose some readers will be unnerved by all this casual talk about directions, and that is understood since most of us now expect detailed GPS coordinates for everywhere we go. This book and its presentation may take a little getting used to if you are one of those who want to alleviate every potential chance of even the slightest error, for those who demand certainty in all of life's endeavors. Well, there is always uncertainty in any cycling journey, as in life, and therein lies the <u>adventure</u> of it all – a voyage of discovery. We discover as we ride! It's more fun.

    For those who yearn for the adventure of uncertainty, who seek out a little challenge of discovery, such as the fellows of the 1804-06 Corps of Discovery (who had <u>NO</u> maps), this book will probably be a good dose of fun and mystery. This will approximate the old days where word of mouth and a bit of common sense and exploration will reveal the way. The first time I rode this route, I never got lost once. It's really that easy.

    Once out onto Highway 101 near MP (milepost) 10, we shall use Oregon Coast Highway (OCH) milepost markers for our guiding signs, which are easy to follow on the road. You will find an OCH MP marker every mile on Hwy 101. They are large.

    So, here we are on OCH heading south towards Gearhart, Seaside, and Cannon Beach. Gearhart appears near MP 19, Seaside near MP 20, and Cannon Beach near MP 28. If you use GPS, and started it at the Clatsop Spit commencement point, you may well find that it is surprisingly close to the OCH MP signs, as the road south from the spit is close in length to where OCH begins Oregon MP markers on the big Astoria-Megler bridge. In any event, now on OCH 101, the MP markers will be our primary factors in determining relative distances between towns and attractions. With roadsigns, the MPs complete the picture. Easy!

Once on OCH 101, it is about 18 miles to Cannon Beach. Using MP markers makes it quick and easy to do mental math as we ride, and it also alleviates any odd issues of odometer error between what may be published in a guidebook and what an individual cyclist's device indicates. They all vary, after all.

Here is the sign you will see as you enter OCH 101 from the ride south of Fort Stevens State Park (if you don't get lost, ha ha). Oregon officially started this bike route in 1982, putting up signs.

For the sake of making things easy, let's use MP markers as our overall mileage, meaning simply that when we arrive in Gearhart, we are about 19 miles into the coastal trip down to the California border. It's close enough – we are here for the ride!

Soon after MP 11 on 101, is a road heading west towards the ocean, just past the Astoria Golf & Country Club. This is Sunset Beach Lane, and for any Lewis and Clark history buffs reading this, the slightly less than a mile diversion here may be in order. Sunset Beach is the trailhead that the expedition used to travel the 6.5 miles from the ocean to Fort Clatsop, during their wet winter stay of 1805-06. There is no camping at Sunset Beach State Park. Nehalem Bay State Park, a popular second night camp, is near MP 43, to give you an idea if you have time to visit Sunset Beach. Much of this depends on your fitness level.

Gearhart (MP 19) offers eating places and grocery stores. It was named after Phillip Gearhart who settled here in the late 1840s. Once the railroad was established around 1889, folks from Portland and Astoria began coming over to picnic and enjoy the coastal scenery. The road through this area is very easy to ride, being primarily flat with wide shoulders. It's relaxed cycling so far, but of course, this won't last, as Arch Cape awaits us south of Cannon Beach. This coastal ride is a string of ups and downs, with memorable scenery to be found at every turn!

Just south of Gearhart, you'll enter the town of Seaside, which is a very popular place for cyclists to explore. Near MP 21, a right turn on Broadway leads to the famous Promenade, full of shops, an aquarium where you can get up close to sea creatures, and a large statue of Lewis and Clark on a beach walkway (a popular place to grab a photo of your bikes, as seen on many CGOAB journals, only 5 blocks off Hwy 101). See this area!

The Lewis and Clark statue sits on the Promenade, with trikes.

Jeremy and Stephanie Bradshaw began their coastal journey in Washington. Here, they enjoy the beach at Seaside's Promenade.

The famous Lewis and Clark tribute in Seaside, Oregon

The Clatsop Tribe was the group of people here when Lewis and Clark's expedition arrived in the very early 1800s. Only about 250 tribal people existed due to the small pox disease introduced by earlier settlers. The Clatsops traded with the Tillamook Tribe to the south, and the Chinook Tribe to the north, across the Columbia River. No bicycles then – they walked.

During the winter of 1805-06, the Corps of Discovery realized they needed more salt to preserve food for their trip back east, so they set up what became known as the salt cairn, or salt works, just north of current-day Seaside. By boiling ocean saltwater here for 18 days, they were able to extract sufficient salt for their expedition needs. These guys were self sufficient.

Now, ya' gotta' be careful when in Seaside however, especially if here at night, as this place is very much **haunted**. The Hotel Seaside, which stood for about a hundred years before being torn down, found several **ghosts** residing there, and after the hotel's demise, they relocated at Girtle's restaurant, a short walk down Broadway. There is a closed room in the kitchen where the **shadow of feet** is often seen walking all around, but there is no body to cast the shadow! Between the kitchen and the dining room, a coffee pot regularly is known to move, and every now and then, even flies across the hallway. The Lil' Bayou restaurant is also similarly abounding with **spirits**, and the owner claims it's an **eerie feeling** when he knows he is being watched in his office. Oh, by the way, the old Hotel Seaside used to sit where the current Shiilo Inn now sits.

Not too far south of Seaside, 101 begins a climb over some hills that separate it from Cannon Beach, which is about 7 miles south. About half way to Cannon Beach, Highway 26 cuts off east to Portlandia, but just remain on 101 of course. This hill will work you! It's an omen of things yet to come your way.

This is the sign after exiting Seaside. Steep hilly riding ahead!

The last 3 miles into Cannon Beach, off Tillamook Head, are all downhill. This is a very quaint little village you'll want to take some time to also explore, for besides all the great shops, market, restaurants, and other attractions, there is the gigantic Haystack Rock, which is an example of a sea stack monolith.

Exit 101 at the sign for **Ecola State Park**, and follow the little streets into town. If you wish to visit Ecola State Park, where you can see the Tillamook Rock lighthouse on out its rock at sea, turn right up the steep hill for a tough ride (may not be worth it for most cyclists, who may already be tired). Once in town, explore to your heart's content. This town is just slightly off 101, but has an easy return when done visiting.

To see Haystack Rock at its closest easy point, take Hemlock Street south until you reach Gower, then turn right on Gower two blocks until it ends at the large motel complexes. It is here that you can pedal right down onto the beach, where you can get a photograph of your bike or trike with Haystack Rock behind you! Haystack Rock is also visible farther south at certain places, but you have to hunt them down. Once you are south of town climbing the grade, you'll also see memorable views of this rock.

We all pedal at our own speeds on overland journeys, and while most coastal cyclists stay at Nehalem Bay State Park this second night, some may feel spent by the time they reach Cannon Beach, which is fine because there are some options for the night here in this cute tourist trap of a town. If you are a motel cyclist, you have many excellent choices, some of which are right here near the Haystack Rock view. If you are a tent camper, there is one option on the south end of town, called *Wright's for Camping*. It is a gorgeous forested setting, however they do not secure their trash cans, therefore there are multiple nightly raccoon invasions! If able, keep pedaling to Nehalem Bay State Park ($6.00 and better showers, instead of Wright's $32.00).

Cannon Beach (MP 28) was named one of the world's most beautiful places in 2013 by National Geographic, and it's easy to see why. This quaint village is 80 miles west of the world's beer capital, which you recall is Portland. The town is 4 miles long, and gets about 750,000 visitors every year, but less than 1800 people call this home. Captain William Clark of the Lewis and Clark expedition was here in 1806.

Main street in Cannon Beach is a happy place, with lots of folks.

In the 1960s, there was a serious sawmill accident. A man was cut to shreds, and despite rapid response and bandaging, he still did not live long. He is locally known as **Bandage Man**, and he still can be found here, an aimlessly roaming **ghost**, forever **haunting** the town of Cannon Beach. His **spirit form** is wrapped totally in smelly old bandages and gauze, and he wanders the outskirts of downtown! For some unknown reason, perhaps just mischievousness resulting from eternal boredom, **Bandage Man** enters cars, and many are the folks who have discovered bloody bandages on their seats. He has also broken windows and dented roofs. Ridiculous as this sounds, **Bandage Man** is also reported to have stolen a Ford Pinto – do they even exist anymore?

Before we head out from Cannon Beach, there is another tale of **haunting** you must hear! Tillamook Rock lighthouse sits atop a rock out in the ocean, off shore of Ecola State Park here. This lighthouse is known as **Terrible Tilly**, and for good reason. It was built on a sea stack, surrounded by depths up to 240 feet. The rock had to be leveled before construction could begin. It was one hazard and issue after another getting Terrible Tilly built.

This tale of **ghosts** is so long and convoluted that to tell it all would necessitate several pages, which we cannot spare, so I'll be brief. You can do further study later for all the details.

     In 1879, the first surveys were attempted prior to the build. The master mason John Trewavas was lost at sea as he attempted to jump onto the huge rock from an unstable boat. He was never found. He was replaced by Charles Ballantyne, who hired a new crew of guys ignorant of what had already occurred, and he kept them sequestered so they would not hear of the tragedy. This crew nearly froze to death during extreme winds one day, and were apparently attacked by sea lions. At last, in January 1881, the lighthouse was finished, with no other deaths.

     Lighthouse keepers had to be hoisted up onto the rock in seas not exactly safe for such maneuvers. Over the years, several lighthouse keepers have reported **bone-chilling screams** while en route up the spiral stairs to the light tower beacon. It is reported that at least two keepers now **haunt** the lone misty sentinel, one friendly, one evil. The evil one had boasted prior to his death that he would kill any future keepers, and when the new keeper arrived at this nearly inaccessible monolith out at sea, the **ghost** attempted to do him in. Chased up the old spiral staircase, the new keeper somehow eluded the **evil one**, but alas, was so shaken by the experience, he had to be removed from service, in a strait jacket! Even he returned, and now is among those **haunting**.

     A **ghost ship** even sails this stretch of Pacific Ocean, having almost run aground on Tillamook Rock in the thick fog that windy night. Several keepers saw the gray form in the mist, but just as it was about to strike the huge rock under the lighthouse, it became calmed, turned around, and sailed away, only the rudder being broken off. Soon after, the broken piece was spotted, but attempts to retrieve it did not meet with success. The Coast Guard never found any evidence of the ship.

     Terrible Tilly was shut down in 1957, but locals still see a dim light at times some nights. Private investors purchased the lighthouse in 1980, converting it into a columbarium (place to store urns of **cremated humans**). Urns had to be transported over by helicopter. The Oregon Mortuary and Cemetery Board revoked the columbarium's license in 1999, due to inaccurate records and issues with human storage procedures. Good night ...

Terrible Tilly, otherwise known on record as the Tillamook Rock lighthouse, sits on Tillamook Rock, about one mile off shore from Ecola State Park and Cannon Beach. After it went dark, a private company purchased it, transforming it into a cemetery at sea, originally designed to hold half a million humans (ash form).

CANNON BEACH TO NEHALEM BAY

This section of the ride is one of the most spectacular of the entire coast, but there are indeed many more that follow! This type of description (spectacular) usually comes about due to a very elevated viewpoint, and you will find it on the incredible Arch Cape/Cape Falcon cliff climbs of Neahkahnie Mountain. These capes are your first big test of gearing. Up, up, and away!

Not far south of Cannon Beach, you will pedal past the first road sign that lets you know how far it is to Manzanita. With all the signs on the roadway, cyclists are never left wondering where they are or how far they have to go to reach the next town.

Past that first road sign is where OCH 101 leaves the flat sandy lands of the beach, where riding was fast and easy, and travels inland over the rugged forested mountains of the Coast Range. This allows us to get to the other side the easiest way possible, because riding along the beach is not an option over the elevated cliffs. You know you are indeed climbing, but until you reach the pullout overlooking Manzanita on the other side, you'll not really realize the full extent of the ascent. It becomes quite apparent, and you'll love the panoramic ocean views. WOW!

So, I call it this first big ascent the Arch Cape hill climb, and it's not too far south of Cannon Beach. If you do choose to spend the night at Cannon Beach (watch out for Bandage Man), you'll be riding up over the top first thing in the morning, when traffic is lighter and air is cooler. There are actually two climbs in this ascent. The first seems like you've reached the summit at the top, because 101 descends, but then you realize it's just like a roller coaster as you begin the second portion of the climb, which is the granddaddy up to the most awesome overlook of the Pacific Ocean you can imagine (at least so far on this trip – there will be others as we ride south). This cape has several more friends, all the way to California of course!

There are two tunnels on the **Oregon Coast Bike Route**, and the first of them you will encounter on the Arch Cape ascent. When you reach the tunnel, you will find a little button just for cyclists to push. So, stop at the little button, make sure your taillight and headlight are on, and then push the little silver button, which activates four bright flashing lights atop the tunnel entrance. They flash two at a time, **diagonally**, and this legally requires car drivers to reduce speed to 30 miles per hour. The tunnel here is well lit inside, with very bright overhead lights, and even if you did not have lights on your bike, you will be seen inside. Some cycle advisors recommend pedaling like a madman.

The cars will pass you, but they are going slow, and yes, there is enough room that experienced cyclists will not be unnerved. Newbies to sharing the road with automobiles might find it a bit spooky though. My advice is to let your fears go, and ride through, because whether the thoughts in your head have you fretting or not, it will make **no** difference in your safety. I pedaled through in a relaxed mode, even taking photos inside, and when I came out the other end, the lights were still flashing on the south side. They flash plenty long for even the slowest among us to pass through. You need **not** pedal like a maniac to survive here! Chill out and live to tell the tale. Opt to **enjoy the tunnel**.

Perhaps counter intuitively, you will actually be **safer** inside this tunnel than on many other curvy portions of 101 where shoulders cease to exist, and curves are somewhat blind to the right. The tunnel flashes the lights, so those evil car monsters will be watching for you! ;-)

Immediately prior to this tunnel, you will be entering Oswald West State Park, which in years prior, provided camping facilities. Now however, this is only a day-use park. Oswald West State Park was named after Oswald West, the man who was instrumental in preserving portions of this beautiful coastline. He was a former governor of Oregon.

Here comes the tunnel – no turning back now!

The tunnel is 1,228 feet long (374 meters), and was built in 1937.

Notice how that large recreational trailer gave me plenty of room.

South of Cannon Beach, an overlook reveals Haystack Rock.

This is one of the views atop the massive cape. Don't look down.

This couple is at Cape Falcon summit. They pedaled a tandem bike up the grade, and also own a microbrewery here in Oregon.

From the dramatic summit, you quickly plunge all the way back down to the ocean far below. It is very steep and fast. The descent is in heavily wooded forest. Prior to the end, you'll see the sign for Manzanita. If you want to turn off 101 here to visit the hillside town, slow down quickly. If not, you still have to hit the binders as you enter the left hand curve into Nehalem.

Just past the final curve is the sign for Nehalem Bay State Park.

From the top of Cape Falcon, we are rewarded for our epic cliff ascent by this incredible view down towards the hillside town of Manzanita. The expanse of the Pacific Ocean to the right of this image is also quite breathtaking. Spend time here. Have a snack!

If you wish to luxuriate prior to climbing Neahkahnie Mountain, you might enjoy staying at this fancy place: 1-800-352-8034

PIRATES, GALLEONS, & BURIED TREASURE!

Manzanita (MP 43), which we just sailed past if we failed to apply the brakes and make the turn into town, is where we find our first **ghosts** who are actually **pirates**! Prepare to be boarded matey if ye dare coast into this haven of **high seas thieves**!

In the late 1500s, long before European settlers arrived in these parts, and more than 200 years prior to the Lewis and Clark expedition, tales by the regional people of the land tell of a large galleon flying a black flag of **skull and crossbones**. Manned by unruly men of dubious character, the ship made land and laid anchor. The Clatsop people were cautious to observe, remaining well hidden on the slopes of Neahkahnie Mountain (which we just pedaled over). What they saw horrified them.

These were real **pirates**, who had recently stolen **chests of gold** from other sailing ships, and they needed a place to stash their booty. At the base of Neahkahnie Mountain, what is now Oswald West State Park, they picked a spot they were sure would safely hide their treasures until they later returned. A notable rock was inscribed to mark the area, and a large pit was dug to contain chests filled with **bullion** and **gold**. Realizing that superstitious people of the land were watching them, and fearful of other **pirates** discovering their treasure before they returned, this band of high seas thieves forced some of their African slaves into the pit to protect the gold filled chests.

The pit was then filled with the excavated dirt and rocks, the slaves being buried alive as insurance that no one would ever attempt to retrieve the gold. The hidden audience of Clatsops saw the ground as now **haunted by spirits** of dead men entrusted to remain guardians. They would not go near this place.

Modern reports leave some area residents occasionally shaken, as it has been reported that piles of stones mysteriously appear overnight, and then just as bizarrely disappear later. Speculation is that the **ghosts** of **lost pirates** are marking the path to where they recall the treasure chests being buried more than 400 years ago, in the hopes that the **ghost galleon** will return to retrieve it someday. Others believe the **spirits** of those slaves buried alive are setting up markers so the rightful heirs of the booty can finally reclaim what belonged to their old ancestors.

Now, about 725 people call Manzanita their year-round home. The name of this town is "little apple" in Spanish, so called due to the numerous Manzanita plants, which have fruit that looks like little apples. At the southern end of Manzanita is Nehalem Bay State Park, which extends to the end of the spit that encloses Nehalem Bay. A spit, also called a sandspit, is a sandy landform that is created by the actions of water, of the ocean and an entering river, such as that found where we began this journey at the Clatsop Spit. Nehalem Bay State Park, which I recommend for spending a night in your tent, is also on a spit.

In 1899, the town of Nehalem (MP 45) was chartered by an act of the legislature. Central to the new town was a tavern, surrounded by other entities, such as saw mill, post office, store, school, and a church to keep all the wild lumber men in check. Once early residents started earning some money, a bank was established to keep it safe, and soon thereafter a railroad linked Nehalem to Portland, as did telephones. Nehalem is also rich farmland, as you'll see as you pedal over the bridge spanning the river that flows into the bay. Fishing was and is another source of income. A dance hall, movie theater, and eateries kept the regional lumber, farm, dairy, and fisher men busy and happy.

If you reach this sign, you've passed Nehalem Bay State Park.

71

The state park sits on a tract of land provided by the county of Tillamook in 1938. The total size today is 895 acres, and the park has an annual overnight attendance of 146,725 campers, some of them hikers and bikers just like us. Pitch your tent, and hope no tsunami visits you tonight!

NEHALEM BAY TO THE LAND OF CHEESE

With the rigors and tales of Arch Cape, Cape Falcon, and Neahkahnie Mountain now behind us, the riding gets easy as we pedal through the towns of Wheeler, Rockaway Beach, and Garibaldi into the world famous cheese and dairy facility in Tillamook. We skirt Nehalem Bay for several miles, ride along the ocean for a bunch more, and then are greeted with fine views as we continue around the very large Tillamook Bay. Along the northern edge of the bay, we can see across to the Three Capes Scenic Loop area where we will be riding after we turn off OCH 101 in the town of Tillamook. This big mass of mountain is also referred to as Cape Meares, and as we have learned, anything with the word "cape" in its name means hill climbing.

There is a great picnic area mid-town, perfect for a snack break.

Wheeler (MP 47) was established by a lumberman named Coleman Wheeler around 1910, and by 1912, he had his lumber mill in full swing. The freight train helped the town along, allowing lumber to be exported. The 1970s saw Wheeler decline economically, but by the early 90s, residents rebounded, working on the area as a tourist oriented locale, a haven for artists, and the center for an arthritis clinic. Aching? Maybe they can help.

But long before this modern development, a fascinating history of **Spanish galleons** and explorers exists. Details are not fully clear, but the accounts are briefly this: In the summer of 1579, **Francis Drake** repaired his ship in this bay. A Spanish galleon is also reported to have wrecked here about the latter 1700s, perhaps the victim of the pirates' high seas thievery. It is also claimed that **Bruno de Heceta**, after whom Heceta Head and the lighthouse north of Florence was named, sailed this area not too long before Lewis and Clark walked and boated from the inland side of the continent. Additionally, from archaeological digs of Nehalem Bay, it is believed that Chinese mariners landed here prior even to first Europeans. Oh, to have seen all that!

South of Wheeler, we can look back northwest to see Neahkahnie Mountain. Visible is the Nehalem River bridge. The ride is easy.

The Old Wheeler Hotel may capture your interest as you pass by, assuming the **ghosts** still continue to support the place. You see, a former owner named Winston Laszlo once took a mind to remodel and refurbish the place, but soon ran into difficulties of the **spooky** kind. He and his wife reported one problem after another from the start. Damage to the hotel was commonplace. Among other **creepy** happenings, one night Winston glimpsed the large mirror in the lobby, to see a gentleman seated in a chair behind him. Startled, Winston looked around, but there was no man in that chair! Other **ghostly** visions had repeatedly been seen during this disturbing time. Ghost hunters were even hired, and it was discovered that bizarre **auras** appeared in camera images. One ghost hunter informed the Laszlo family that it is not at all unusual for haunting spirits to be unsettled during times of change or reconstruction, and they rebel at the process. And, in keeping with **ghost** behaviors, as well as behaviors of the living, once a point of acceptance is reached, the apparitions settle down and happily exist with it all.

Back to the bike trip now, after passing where Nehalem Bay flows into the Pacific Ocean, we arrive in a flat sandy land that has a town called Rockaway Beach (MP 51). Here the OCH 101 becomes a cyclist's worst nightmare, at least as far as paving is concerned. Even though the road is flat and fast, the ride is anything but comfy, as the rough chip sealed surface seems like it will surely loosen the fillings in your teeth. Mile after mile of this shaking will have you cursing the route!

We pass Twin Rocks State Park, a small beachside diversion, and then Smith Lake, before the road enters Barview, which has a place where you can pitch a tent if you wish. The Barview County Park is signed, but without exception, every cyclist I've talked to has told me that this campground is less than acceptable, compared to the nice state parks, so, based on this emphatic advice, usually expressed in language I best not repeat here, I didn't even stop to check it out.

Somewhere after Rockaway Beach, the precise location or MP marker no longer recalled due to my brain reaching a numbed state of forgetfulness from the horrible road surface, we finally enter another tiny rural town called Garibaldi, which gives the impression of a richer town experience.

An afternoon fog covers Tillamook Bay and Barview Park.

Garibaldi (MP 55) has a unique beginning. In 1856, Charley Farwell took up residence on this bayside ground. He had asked to be left behind when the ship he was serving on docked here. Mister Farwell was a deckhand on the Calumet, and the captain agreed to let him go. This was only forest. An old diary says he built himself a "snug house" where Garibaldi now stands. His plan was to become a "bar pilot" here.

Daniel Bayley really got things hopping however. As the first significant property owner, he began subdividing the land, and built a hotel and store. In 1870, he was appointed by US president Ulysses S. Grant as the first postmaster of the area. Daniel was told to name this place for the record, so he named it after a hero of his, a fellow named Giuseppe Garibaldi, who was helping to unify Italy and do his part for spreading democracy wherever he could in the world. Thus, it's a hero's town.

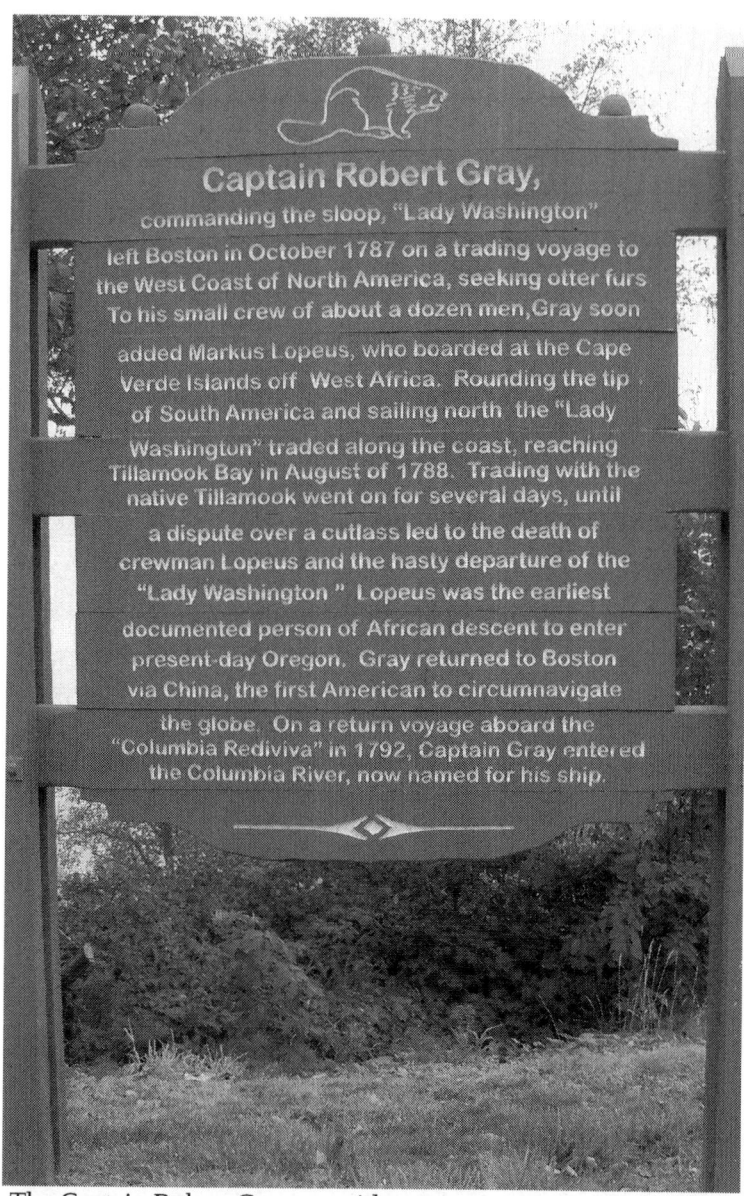

The Captain Robert Gray wayside appears as you enter the small town of Garibaldi, and tells about his ship, the Lady Washington.

A replica of Robert Gray's Lady Washington sails the Pacific Coast today, making appearances and giving tourists hour rides.

Daniel and Giuseppe would be proud to see all us cyclists riding through this little bayside town. It is very quaint and relaxing.

There it is, looming the full length of the main street through town! The monolithic stack is a treasured landmark nowadays.

In 1921, a place called the Whitney Mill opened, and in 1927, the Hammond Company constructed a tall smoke stack as part of this operation on the east side of town. Today, as you pedal through here, you can't help but notice this tall landmark, loved by some because of its history, despised by others for spoiling the natural landscape. Why is it still here?

As with several Oregon coastal towns, Garibaldi has roots in the deforestation business, using the resulting lumber to power the area financial successes. Where lumber mills exist, population grows. The town's population grew to more than 1,500 residents in the 1950s because the Oceanside Lumber Company and the Oregon-Washington Plywood Corporation provided work. The only mill today is owned by Weyerhaeuser, which operates out of the Port of Garibaldi.

Once past the old crumbling smoke stack, the road regains its rural country feel as it rounds an inlet of Tillamook Bay, and then curves around to the left, with great views of the bay, and Cape Meares on the other side. The riding remains easy and as fast as you like to pedal. The nine miles or so into the Tillamook Land of Cheese are all along this bay waterfront.

A wheelchair bound man examined my "wheelchair" for quite a long time, both before and after he got his groceries in Garibaldi.

Cape Meares is clearly visible across the immense Tillamook Bay, off to the southwest. The Cape Meares lighthouse sits up there, and is on our route, which leaves 101 at First Street in Tillamook, onto what is called the Three Capes Scenic Loop. For your Oregon Coast ride to truly count, you **must** take this loop!

Don't miss the Tillamook Cheese Factory at MP 64. See the ship!

80

Take your photo with the Baby Loaf miniature van in the lobby!

Tillamook is known for far more than just black and white dairy cows and their products, which, by the way, are all free of rBST and the nasty other growth hormones typically added to cows of most dairy products. Yes, you can indulge in Tillamook dairy delights with a happy heart! Say cheese!

What is now known as Tillamook, named in honor of the Tillamook tribal people who originally lived in these parts when Europeans began to arrive, was the location of the first landing on the Oregon Coast. Tillamook is an Indian word meaning "the many peoples of the Nehelim". Captain Robert Gray, in charge of the American sloop Lady Washington, put anchor here in this bay, believing he had found a great river to the west. This landing occurred on August 14, 1788, sixteen years prior to the arrival of the Lewis and Clark expedition. Most believed a large river flowed clear across the continent, including Thomas Jefferson.

1851 marked the year of the first white settlement in the area. Joseph Champion found a hollow old spruce tree and called it his castle. By 1853, an act of the legislature created Tillamook County. More folks kept on settling here. By 1854, the growing community began construction of a ship they called the Morning Star to help aid in their movement of dairy and other supplies. Shipping accidents had destroyed all the other vessels, and this ship was built to remedy those losses. Iron for this great boat was hauled by horse over Neahkahnie Mountain (remember what we just pedaled up and over?), which was salvaged from a shipwreck north of there. It becomes clear why lighthouses were eventually built along the rugged Oregon Coast, with many crashing ships!

TILLAMOOK TO PACIFIC CITY

This portion of our ride will be one of the most memorable, as it spans **three** magnificent capes along the way. We depart OCH, so I'll not be discussing the milepost markers for the next 30+ miles. This cape route will demonstrate even to mileage devotees that simply enjoying the road without fear of getting lost is a fun thing – especially on this coastal trek. Just let the adventure unfold.

101 is Main Street once the city limit of Tillamook is entered. You will see a brown sign with white letters saying CAPE MEARES, with a lighthouse icon above it. This sign is at First Street, where you will tun west. It's time to depart the coast highway. We will be on Highway 131 for the beginning of our ride over to the gorgeous cape area. It is very well signed, so don't worry – you will not get lost ! At every bend, there is a sign. And at bike or trike speeds, it is not possible to miss these signs.

The Cape Meares sign appears at First Street, and this is where most riders turn west to catch Highway 131. You can also ride south to Third Street, which actually is Highway 131, but turning at First gets you off the main street sooner, and onto residential streets. There are signs at every curve. It's truly easy!

This view is looking back east towards Tillamook once on the road to Cape Meares. It is early morning around sunrise, on a partly cloudy day. The views are relaxing and agricultural here.

Every turn and bend is very well signed all the way to the capes.

You have options when you reach this split. <u>Both</u> ways take you to Cape Lookout State Park, but going left does so more directly because it bypasses Cape Meares, the lighthouse, Oceanside, and Netarts. Turn **RIGHT** here, to Cape Meares! It's **THE** route!

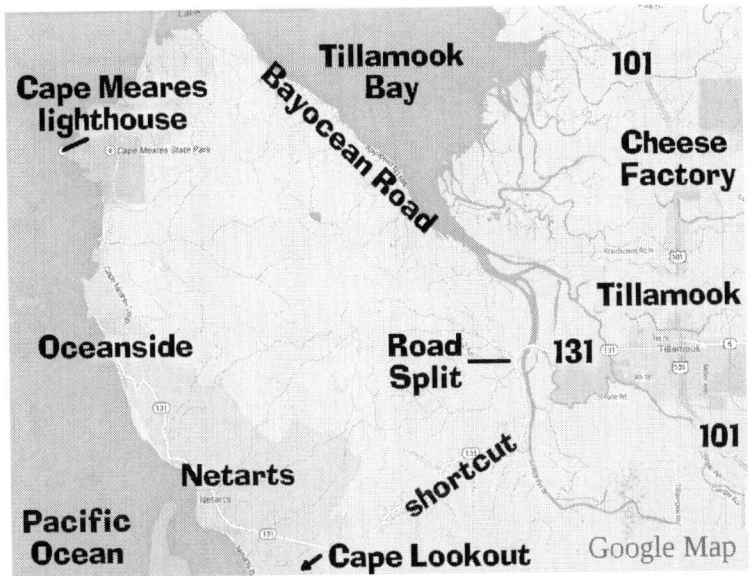

EXPLANATION OF MAP: This appears harder than it really is. The road split is where you turn right to ride along Tillamook Bay, on Bayocean Road. Out towards the north end of the cape, Bayocean Road curves left at Cape Meares Lake, and a little less than a quarter mile farther, Bayshore Drive takes you up the forested mountain to Cape Meares State Park and the lighthouse (*It's the shortest lighthouse on the coast – worth seeing*). From there, it goes down to the small towns of Oceanside and Netarts.

From Netarts, remain on Netarts Bay Drive (which changes to Netarts Bay Road, also known as Whiskey Creek Road) until you reach Cape Lookout Road, which will take you back up the mountain to Cape Lookout State Park and the summit. At the summit, there is a large parking area to the right for the Cape Lookout trailhead. Most cyclists will opt not to take this long hike, but it goes out to the very end of a weird finger of mountain that juts out into the Pacific Ocean – way WAY out!

Anyway, this explanation is becoming rather confusing if you are not familiar with this loop, but as mentioned, the signs along the way will make it all unmistakably clear, and you'll end up saying: "That was easy!" Look this up on Google Earth also.

The Cape Meares lighthouse is very short because it's on a cliff.

This is the famous Octopus Tree near the lighthouse. Don't miss!

The Cape Meares lighthouse resides on a 200 foot cliff. It was lit in January 1890 by the first keeper, Anthony Miler. Light was provided by a fire-wick kerosene lamp, and shined through red and clear glass lenses. It can be seen 21 miles out to sea.

A short walk takes you to the largest Sitka Spruce tree in Oregon.

The Cape Meares cliffs are spectacular, and not to be missed!

The Three Capes road has lots of Steep Hilly Intense Terrain!

Cape Lookout State Park campground is in a gorgeous setting, south of Cape Meares lighthouse. This is prior to the big climb.

Only in the weird state of Oregonia could one possibly imagine a sign cautioning bicyclists about **S**teep **H**illy **I**ntense **T**errain. Does this really exist out here on the cape loop? Well, I suppose you will just have to ride the roads until you find this last sign.

This sign is located on the shortcut road that splits to the left back there where the other goes to Cape Meares. This is not part of the official **Oregon Coast Bike Route**, so you will not see this exact sign as you hug the bay, ocean, and headlands. This shortcut is inland, with **none** of the spectacular views of the official route.

91

This cliff overlook is where Dick Gammon (1943-2009) jumped off many years ago. He was a pioneering hang glider pilot, and this very scenic point is called Gammon Launch in his honor. It's a great place to hang glide due to the water and sandy beach far below. Notice the mountains we've ridden to the distant north.

The beach in the background is how far out over the ocean I have hiked on the trail to this end point. This extremely narrow finger of land is readily visible from **150** kilometers in space (**93** miles). This utterly amazing earth-form is about a mile and a half long!

Looking south: Cape Lookout road summit, at 839 feet, is the highest elevation we attain on the **Oregon Coast Bike Route**!

This is the intersection at the bottom of the long steep downhill coming off of Cape Lookout. There is a stop sign here. **Do not** continue straight to Highway 101 here, or you will miss seeing the final cape on this loop, Cape Kiwanda (recall this is the Three Capes Scenic Route, and you have already seen two of them thus far). **Turn right** at the stop sign and ride to Pacific City instead. You will be rejoining Highway 101 later, after Pacific City. This is Sandlake Road, with three camping options. The ride is easy.

If you want to straddle a different type of vehicle for a while, it's your lucky day, but it will cost you fifty-five smackers per hour!

This is the type of detailed signing you will find all along this Three Capes Scenic Loop. Also, you will usually see the **OREGON COAST BIKE ROUTE** sign quite frequently at intersections – it is green with white lettering. This particular sign array is located on the Sandlake road, heading south, and is 3 miles north of Pacific City, which has a market if you need food.

A solo female biker, pedaling to San Francisco, California from Seattle, Washington, rides over Cape Kiwanda to Pacific City.

　　Well, if Cape Lookout State Park is really windy and cold the afternoon you arrive, stay here instead. One biker told me recently that even in her tent and sleeping bag, it was so cold on that September night that she was doubting the camping decision Anyway, there are options, such as the Cape Kiwanda Inn down the hill in Pacific City. You don't have to rough-it! Take it easy.

Cape Lookout State Park is an expansive and beautiful setting on the rugged Oregon Coast. It is not to be missed on your cycling trip. The U.S. Lighthouse Service presented 975 acres on the cape to Oregon in 1935 for use as a state park. Over the years, more land was acquired to expand this park, which was initially left undeveloped as a natural preserve, and Sam Boardman, the first State Parks Superintendent, was inclined to limit the use to the lookout trail, where you saw me standing in that photo.

Work to expand the scenic park began in 1952, and the campground was opened in '54. Tillamook County put in a road to this cape and on down to Sandlake in the late 1960s. Today, the park acreage amounts to 2,014, and the annual overnight attendance is more than 112,000 excited touring folks. In August 1943, a B-17 bomber crashed into the cape, and it required a full day for rescuers to reach the only surviving crewman.

Sand Lake Recreation Area is a natural estuary, north of Pacific City. The U.S. Forest Service has three camping solutions here, which are open all year: East Dunes, West Winds, and Sand Beach. It is warmer down here than up at the cape camground.

As the common story goes, there were long-established tribal communities in this area prior to being edged out by incoming folks who wished to settle here. In 1886, a salmon cannery was built at what is now called Pacific City. Logging, fishing, and dairy interests began to expand, and with them came vacationers. Early visitors had a two day ride to Pacific City in horse and buggy vehicles. Many had never seen an ocean before, having traveled out west on the Oregon Trail from inland portions of the country. With this influx of tourists came ways to house them during their visit, and thus Pacific City grew touristy.

Ocean Park was the original name of Pacific City, but it was changed in 1909 to avoid confusion with another town of the identical name in Washington. Thomas Brooten discovered a special ore he told others had healing properties, and he built a resort in 1904 to attract folk who had ailments and were looking for cures. He put sick people into baths of the ore, and fed it to them by mouth. For a few years, the Kelp Ore Resort saw a booming business, but a tuberculosis outbreak was its undoing. Brooten Road, which we will ride from Pacific City back out to rejoin OCH 101 was named after this interesting man.

The First Inhabitants of Oregon's coastal areas fished for food.

Totem pole at the Umpqua Discovery Center, Reedsport

PACIFIC CITY TO LINCOLN CITY

At the south end of Pacific City are signs that will readily direct you back out to Highway 101, which we have happily not missed during our incredible ride on the Three Capes Scenic Loop. It's almost too bad we have to rejoin all the automobile traffic, but we'll get in some quick and easy miles to Lincoln City – that is, until we reach Cascade Head, over which we must pedal. It's one of those Steep Hilly Intense Terrain affairs (more SHIT), but it's only about two miles long, and the ride down the other side is a yahoo "full speed ahead" thrill.

Having pedaled east on Brooten Road from Pacific City, an easy and scenic stretch of road, we arrive at this sign when we roll up to the stop sign at Oregon Coast Highway 101. It was wise we avoided 101 from Tillamook to here, because there is one right hand blind curve that has no shoulder and is VERY concerning for cyclists wishing to remain alive. Big trucks drive out there.

Kayakers enjoy the Little Nestucca River, south of Brooten Road.

Our route is lower in elevation now, and there are no sea stacks. Above, we see Daley Lake on our way towards Neskowin. Neskowin (MP 98) has about 170 residents. Slab Creek empties into the Pacific Ocean here, on the town's beach, and Proposal Rock (wanna' get married) is at the south end of town, before the road climbs Cascade Head, on the 13 mile ride to Lincoln City.

Okay, here you will want to remain on 101, despite that the state has signed the **OREGON COAST BIKE ROUTE** to turn left onto the Old Hwy 101 route (MP 99), which was used prior to the new road over Cascade Head. The old road is shady and hardly has any cars, but it's also longer, curvy, shoulderless and more effort. Most cyclists just keep on pedaling straight here.

Just beyond the Old Hwy 101 turn-off sign, begins the long ascent over Cascade Head. We enter the Siuslaw National Forest here. If your bike is geared properly, this is no big deal. If not, get off and push it. It seems long on a bike or trike, however it is not really difficult to ride. The highway is pretty wide open on this stretch. It's time to climb to the 761 foot summit now.

Cascade summit is really 761 feet, then free-fall to Lincoln City!

After your screaming and wild white-knuckled descent off Cascade Head, you'll soon be entering the final easy miles into Lincoln City, one of the coast's premier places to visit. This interchange in the photo (MP 105) exists because Highway 18 comes into 101 here from Portland, and the volume of traffic demanded such an efficient road melding. Of course, this means be extra careful on a bike or trike. The off-ramp above is not so bad, but around that corner up there is an on-ramp, where you can get creamed if negligent! That's where I got killed (I'm a ghost).

Wow, now this is very cool! This sign (MP 112) appears in the tiny town of Neotsu, where I used to live when I taught at the middle school. This is just about a quarter mile before hitting Lincoln City, but the bummer is that the sign is only facing northbound traffic, so you gotta' know it's there if you want your own photograph (which hardly any cyclist ever gets because they don't know about it). Just after you pass the Neotsu post office on your left, at the Devil's Lake road, 101 hits a downgrade, and that is where this sign lives. There's a golf course up on the right.

Coastal Safeway supermarkets provide all the grub you'll need.

You're probably going want some food before you check in to Devil's Lake State Park this evening, primarily because the small market back in Neskowin is really very minimalistic, and has mostly a bunch of junk food for tourists in a big hurry, not serious cycle bums like us who need serious nutrition!

Okay, so you've just pedaled past the large golf course at the 45th parallel sign, past the Lincoln City limit sign and now you are climbing a hill to a congested intersection with a traffic light. You will want to turn right at the light, which is **Logan Road**. You'll know it because on the opposite side of 101 is a Mc Donald's junk food café, but if you attempt to turn left into the McBurger, you'll get flattened by a mess of cars, so forget the idea! Anyway, the **Safeway** supermarket is just up Logan Road a few yards on the left, in a large shopping center. It is easy to miss this market because it sits back up off the highway a bit.

Devil's Lake State Park (MP 114) is on the southwestern edge of Devil's Lake, and the little river that flows from Devil's Lake into the big ocean is the shortest river on Planet Earth (120 feet). If you cross the bridge on the World's Shortest River, go

105

back a couple blocks for your camping at Devil's Lake State Park. The park is small, only 109 acres, receiving about 34,000 campers each year, but it's only a walk across 101 to be on the huge sandy beach where the big kite festivals are held every year in Lincoln City. Those are awesome to watch!

Lincoln City (MP 112) is a town that receives a lot of tourism business from Portlandia, Salem, and all the huge metro areas over east in the Willamette Valley, so on weekends, this fun ocean town can be quite crowded. Parts of the town have no ideal place for cyclists to ride, but since most of it is two lanes in each direction, I just use the car lane, but if this is uncomfortable for you, simply hop up on the sidewalks in the really narrow places. This town has about 7 miles of beaches.

The region was explored by Europeans in the 1500s, with folks from England, France, Portugal, and Spain sailing around in the ocean seeking a passage through what is now called America. None of them were successful at locating it however, because it did not exist. This area was named New Albion by Francis Drake, who sailed his ship here in 1572. August 1837 saw the first tourists of record. By 1855, the United States began sequestering the original first inhabitants (know commonly as Indians) onto reservations, eventually restricting them to the Siletz Reservation. In 1887, the US Congress passed an act that allowed white folks to have part of the reservation lands, restricting to 80 acre parcels that which the first people could have. Same old story.

Fishing was a prevailing industry early-on, but by the 1920s, the aquatic animals were being fished out, and by 1935, new law made sure certain types of fishing were proclaimed illegal. Logging then began to grow, as it did in many other coastal regions, and today it is common to see huge clear-cut areas while on OCH 101. The common trend was that once the new settlers entered a region, all the resources were rather rapidly diminished. Prior to white immigration, the lands along the coast were in a natural state, as described frequently by the first settlers in their written journals. In less than 200 years however, all that has dramatically changed. Of course, without that change, we wouldn't be cycling today along this beautiful coast!

Oh, and yes, there are **hauntings** that are alive and well in Lincoln City too! During the 1950s, a firefighter suffered a fatal stroke, and now his **ghost** continues to wander with abandon around the fire station and its grounds. South of town is Siletz Bay, and there are many reports by regional folks about a schooner that sails the bay still. This **ghost ship** simply appears in the fog, sails along for a while, and then is enveloped once again in the mist, and no one knows quite why. As with other bays and waterways along the Oregon Coast, many shipwrecks have occurred over the decades, as the captains making poor judgments ran their ships aground, or crashed them onto rocks. One is known to be buried in the mudflats of Siletz Bay, and was visible until the 1980s. In 2001, a lady who lives on the bay reported seeing this **phantom ship** maneuvering full speed towards her living room window, but then, as always, vanished into nothingness just prior to coming ashore.

Just off Highway 101 on the left side, a bit past MP 114, you'll see a sign pointing left at the signal for Devil's Lake State Park. A small two-level hiker/biker camp is here, and a short walk on a little path takes you to wonderful warm showers in a modern bath facility with all the luxuries!

This couple from Poland were taking a short afternoon rest here. People from all over this planet flock to ride this scenic route!

Having registered at Devil's Lake State Park, and feeling happy about the 60+ miles I had ridden that day, I met a fellow who made my physical endeavor seem mild by comparison!

Now here's a fellow who really knows what it's like to be on the road for a very long time compared to what I am used to, and for a journey that would take me less than three months on my human powered trike, he is spending close to two years doing! This sign was strapped to the rear of Stephen's backpack, and is what initially drew me to meet him. It's a lot slower walking than pedaling, and probably a lot harder too! You can visit his website at: http://www.stephensadventure.com

Stephen Hnilica sits at our community picnic table in Lincoln City, with bicyclist Amanda Alexander preparing dinner while cell phone chatting. Stephen was walking from Tampa, Florida to Seattle, Washington to educate 10,000 Kids in India. When on an Oregon coastal cycling tour, you will meet all kinds of fascinating folks along the way! It's always fun to check into the hiker/biker camping areas early so you have plenty of time to chat with everyone who is out there pedaling or walking the coast. One reason I really enjoy camping at these hiker/biker campgrounds in state parks is that I meet many interesting people, and have loads of fun discussions, things that I would never experience if I stayed in expensive motels each night.

WHY CYCLISTS REALLY LOVE OREGON

There is a big reason why the Oregon Coast is considered the best of the Pacific Coast ride. It is indeed a very BIG reason, and you'll know it's big when you approach it, and pedal up it. I just wanted to cover a little geology lesson about capes and heads.

Cape derives from a Latin work meaning head, that being the word caput. Capes and heads are large promontories of land, also called headlands, that jut out into the ocean, sometimes a little way, sometimes a long way, but always they share one thing: their height compared to the surrounding sandy beaches below.

Now, some folks get all entangled in debates about what some points of land are called. They are the technophiles who stumble over word meanings to such an extreme level that they will tell you such stuff like *"Cape Perpetua isn't really a cape!"* Okay, but my thoughts indicate that it really doesn't matter. For cyclists, these headlands are what make Oregon the best. They satisfy our addiction! Cape or head, who cares? It's the ride over the headlands that keep cyclists coming back for more each year!

Cape Perpetua, as viewed from Yachats, on the central coast.

A line of bicyclists approach the final few yards of the summit at Cape Falcon, on Neahkahnie Mountain, past Arch Cape. This spectacular portion is one of the favorites enjoyed by all cyclists.

LINCOLN CITY TO NEWPORT

Okay, now back to the riding of the route – intermission over! Lincoln City to Newport is some very enjoyable mileage, much of which is quite easy, and fast if you wish to crank along for a bit. Getting one's cardio system pumped from rapid forward movement can be fun! Yee Haa ...

This huge painting on the side of an old brick building will jump out at you after departing Devil's Lake State Park and crossing the world's shortest river. Past this painting, at the top of a small hill, will be the Factory Outlet Stores, a trap for touring motorists, but not for cyclists. We can't carry a bunch of gifts in our bags!

Just past MP 120, we cross a bridge over the Siletz River, making good time pedaling around Siletz Bay towards Gleneden Beach State Park, which is a day use area off 101. About 5 miles south of the inviting Salishan Golf Course complex at Gleneden Beach, just prior to Government Point, we arrive at Boiler Bay State Scenic Viewpoint. I definitely recommend a stop and rest here at Boiler Bay! This is a huge area on the ocean side, with immense grass lawns, picnic tables, paved walkways, restrooms, and incredible photogenic overlooks of the waves crashing on the rocks down below. The reason this is called Boiler Bay is because in 1910, a cargo ship, called the *J. Marhoffer,* sank here. At low tide, the ship's boiler is still visible, as it is slowly being consumed by the sand over the years.

Once back on the highway, it's just a short jaunt south to the tiny and quaint little coastal village of Depoe Bay (MP 127), a place that invites every cyclist to stop for some photos along the seawall. The tiny harbor, believed to be the smallest navigable harbor on Planet Earth (six *acres*), was once home to the first people of the region who hunted seal and fish here. This land was taken from the original inhabitants by the United States, and the country placed them on a coastal reservation. Historical accounts vary, but one indicates that the name of the town derived from a Siletz tribal member called Charlie Depot. The family changed the spelling to Depoe in 1928, and then government opened a post office using that name on their records. So it stuck.

About 1200 people live here all year long. Nowadays, tourism is a key component of Depoe Bay's existence, with cute little shops all along the short stretch of minuscule downtown. During certain times of weather and ocean activity, some colossal waves crash into, and high above, the town's little seawall, splashing all over parked cars and any pedestrians who happen to be walking along! It is quite dramatic to witness.

The seawall in Depoe Bay can be a very wet place at times!

Pirates Cove is about a quarter mile north of this Pirate Coffee Company in Depoe Bay. If you like pirate oriented gifts, this is your place! Get your photo with that pirate behind my trike.

See how friendly pirates can be? This cyclist is the gal on the cover of this book, and we rode together for a couple of days. You always meet other happy bikers on the road. Join up now!

A cool coffee mug for sale at the Pirate Coffee Company.

The world's smallest harbor is signed, so get this unique photo while you are pedaling through. It's the only one on the planet!

Exiting south from Depoe Bay, we pick up speed once again and soon reach Whale Cove, and then after skirting around the small inlet, we arrive at Rocky Creek State Scenic Viewpoint, which is very similar to Boiler Bay. Take some time to relax here, take some pictures of Whale Cove and crashing waves, and then prepare to depart Highway 101 once again, on a short diversion that you absolutely **MUST** take because it is **our official route!**

You may find this alternate route mentioned in some best selling coastal cycling book, but it is usually just as an aside note about **Cape Foulweather**. Sure, you can remain on OCH 101, climb the huge hill with plenty of high speed automobile traffic on a narrow shoulder, and see nothing but forest, but why would you choose to do so? This **Otter Crest Loop** will blow you away with its private feel, practically no cars at all, single lane devoted to cyclists, and some of the **best** cliff views of the Pacific Ocean you can imagine anywhere! It hugs the mountainside called Cape Foulweather the entire way, and exits back onto 101 not far north of Beverly Beach State Park, where many of us end up camping.

The cycling route on Otter Crest Loop!

WOW

This is the little gift shop at the summit point, 462 feet above sea level, on Cape Foulweather. You can't even hear OCH 101 at all.

At the south side of the little parking lot at the gift shop is a southerly overlook, which reveals this incredible panorama! That is the **Inn at Otter Crest** down below, a wonderful place to stay if you want to get inside for a luxurious overnight and a fine restaurant. The flat beach in the distance is back on 101, and is where Beverly Beach State Park is located, where you can camp in woods across from the sea, and get hot showers, for only $6.00 per cyclist. State parks are my **number one** option for camping!

Beverly Beach State Park, south of Cape Foulweather, sits on Spencer Creek, and sees an overnight attendance annually of more than 148,000 people. The park sits on 135 acres.

The cycling shoulder from Beverly Beach SP on south into Newport is quite wide, flat and fast, and full of excellent views of the ocean, where you can stop to get photos. This section of highway is also subject to the moving of the ground on a fairly regular basis, thus you'll notice large slabs of older highway that are all jutted up and wrecked. Apparently the wet weather during the winter wreaks havoc on this stretch of ground.

As you ride along south of Beverly Beach, you will notice off in the distance to the southwest a very tall white lighthouse with a beam that seems to flash frequently. The farther towards Newport you ride, the more obvious it becomes when you're out in the open. This is the Yaquina Head lighthouse, and it was built in 1873. It is Oregon's **tallest** light beacon on this coast, at 93 feet in height! It is contained within the Yaquina Head Outstanding Natural Area, which requires a fee. Entry to this area is about 3 miles south of Beverly Beach State Park. If you wish to visit it, you'll have to ride a mile west onto the headland, at the intersection where Izzy's Pizza sits at the northwest corner.

Back in the 1990s, the red roof of Izzy's Pizza was blown off by a winter storm, where wind reached speeds of 120 miles per hour! This lighthouse was built to withstand these elements of weather, and thus still stands. While this lighthouse was being built, two ships crashed on the headlands. In 1920 lightning hit this tower, but did not damage it. After all these years, it is but one vertical inch off perfect vertical! The builders knew their craft well. This is a very stately lighthouse you would enjoy seeing up close.

This is the first Newport sign you will see, which is quite a ways north of what seems to be the actual town. There is a lot here if you are seeking a place to hang out for a while, or partake of fine dining. Newport – The **bike shop** has both Wi-Fi and laundry!

Newport, Oregon (MP 141), is one of the coast's most popular towns for visitation. As with Lincoln City 25 miles to the north, access to the coast via popular roads from Oregon's central Willamette Valley allow high volumes of "inlanders" to invade the place. Of course, local businesses laugh all the way to the bank! Tourists began coming here in 1856, and they just never stopped. In fact, today it's so popular that Oregon has signed an alternate path through the traffic over along the beach if you prefer things quieter and slower. Even with its popularity however, Newport is no metro area, and can definitely be ridden through on a bike or trike. Why would one wish to do this? Well, there are things like big Safeway supermarkets, Fred Meyer superstores, bicycle shops, and laundromats in all this relative hubbub. So here, you must decide what your priorities are, and seek the appropriate pathway. And yes, you can do it all.

If you need to shop at Safeway, it's on the north end of town on the left hand side of the road, but it is south of where the official bike route turns off for the quieter beach areas. There is also a Walmart about a block before you get to Safeway, on the right side of the road. You can stop at these places, and then cut over back streets to the west to rejoin the bike route if you wish. Since the bike route essentially hugs the ocean, and is only a few blocks west, you can't end up going too far west or miss it. In other words, at any place in Newport, if you peel off Highway 101 and head west, any road you take out there at the beach will eventually feed back into 101 prior to the Yaquina Bay bridge.

On the **Oregon Coast Bike Route** alternate along the beach, there are a few small stores, and when you get to the southern portion of the town, there will be a small sign that tells you to turn left to access the **bicycle shop** (NW 6 St) if you need bike repair or parts . There is also a laundry **and** internet right **IN** the bike shop (it's your lucky day! ;-) Can't beat that!

This is a commercial laundromat, not the one in the bike shop. Sooner or later, all cyclists have to do the dreaded laundry stop!

Turn here to remain on the bike route through Newport.

Agate Beach Wayside, looking north to Yaquina Head lighthouse.

The Agate Beach Wayside is an Oregon State Park day use facility, which occupies just over 18 acres of beach. About 190,000 people visit this beach yearly as part of their Newport experience. From the parking lot, there is a pedestrian tunnel that goes to the ocean. Surfing and clamming are popular activities.

This is the Yaquina Bay lighthouse, differentiated from the Yaquina Head lighthouse, which is north of Newport. This lighthouse is just prior to crossing the Yaquina Bay bridge.

The Yaquina Bay lighthouse lived and worked for only a very short time as an actual lighthouse. It was first lit for service in 1871, but folks had been arguing, saying it should have been built on Yaquina Head instead. Well, in 1873, the Yaquina Head lighthouse went up, and by 1874, Yaquina Bay lighthouse went dark for good. But that's not the end of the story! Read on, but first make sure you are safe under the covers ...

Born in the late 1800s, Muriel Travenard was one day dropped off in Newport by her dad, a sea captain, to visit her friends. Well, she and her buddies decided to go explore the area, and ended up at what was by then an abandoned lighthouse that was no longer in service. The group of teen aged girls continued walking around the area, when Muriel realized she must have left her scarf on the white picket fence at the lighthouse. So, she begged a moment's pardon, took leave of her friends, and quickly ran back to get the scarf. After a reasonable amount of time had passed, her friends became very concerned because Muriel had not yet returned to the group, so they all walked back over to find her. She should have easily been back by now, they thought.

Walking around the abandoned lighthouse as evening was coming on, they called out her name, but received no answer. Soon, they became **scared**, frantically running around searching for her, but to no avail. One of them suggested they look inside the door, which they did, and then discovered a pool of **fresh blood** on the floor. Despite the quick intervention of adults subsequent to this **gruesome discovery**, the young lady was never found. What actually happened to poor Muriel remains a true mystery to this very day.

You can still see this old stain on the floor if you visit the old lighthouse, which was originally going to be torn down a few times over the years, but was finally saved and renovated in 1974 by the Oregon State Park Group. Also, still today, some folks report seeing Muriel as she peers aimlessly from the lantern room of Yaquina Bay lighthouse, as if trying to locate her friends from so long ago. There are others who swear Muriel has been seen walking the pathways of the lighthouse grounds. Word also has it Coast Guard servicemen have experienced a few **unexplainable** situations around the old abandoned lighthouse. Yes, the **ghost** of Muriel lives on, as do they all here on the Oregon Coast!

So, there you have it – another fascinating reason to ride the official **Oregon Coast Bike Route** along the beach area, which also is the original oceanfront resort area of old Newport in its early days, called the **Nye Beach Historic District**. This lighthouse sits overlooking a grand view of the Pacific Ocean too, with picnic tables and walkways if you need to stretch before pedaling over the big bridge to South Beach State Park for a night of camping. The Nye Beach Historic District also allows you access to the beach area between the two lighthouses here.

After pedaling back out onto 101, we are immediately presented with the ultra mega huge Yaquina Bay bridge, called by many the Newport bridge. This will strike fear into the hearts of quite a few bikers and trikers who first lay eyes upon it! So, I have personally gone out and walked the entire bridge with a tape measure in hand to verify that there is PLENTY of room on the sidewalk for the widest cyclist. The narrowest the walkway becomes anywhere is 41 wonderful inches, and it is actually wider in several areas. The apex is near the north shore, so it's possible to ride the lane southbound (foolish to try northbound). By remaining on the sidewalk, you can totally relax and enjoy the view and experience! Why have to pedal like a maniac, after all?

Here is a view from my eyes while pedaling my fully loaded tricycle over the Yaquina Bay bridge. I easily fit on the sidewalk with plenty of lateral room to spare, and I'm on a trike with bags!

Once over the colossal bridge, you'll pass the Hatfield Marine Science Center and the Oregon Coast Aquarium facilities, both off to the left side of the highway, covering a huge acreage. These are grand places to visit if you are going to spend some extra time in the Newport area, and I highly recommend them to you! Both sit on the shore of the bay. Also, Newport's Old Town is quite quaint and fun (north side of bridge), with things like *Ripley's Believe it or Not* museum (okay, it's REALLY weird, but you might like it). And, if that's not enough, there are usually giant sea lions lying around all over the wooden docks in Old Town, and you can hear them often when riding into that section, sounding like a pack of wild dogs barking.

By the way, if you ever saw the movie called *Free Willy* years ago, about an orca whale who was kept in captivity and then released in to the open ocean, the Oregon Coast Aquarium is where the main actor, Willy, used to reside while awaiting return to the wild seas. The whale's actual human-given name was **Keiko**, and thousands of people came to this aquarium every year for several years to see him in his gigantic tank of salt water. Keiko was released in real life in 1998, loaded onto a US Air Force C-17 cargo plane in a special huge container, and airlifted to Westman Islands in Iceland, where he was then freed into his natural waters. Unfortunately, Keiko's return was ultimately unsuccessful, and he died in 2003 of pneumonia.

After the Oregon Coast Aquarium, we begin heading out of town, and towards South Beach State Park for those of you who want a great campground with hot showers. There is also a relatively new motel just over the bridge on the left side for those who want a night of very pampered luxury – in fact, if you wish to visit the famous Oregon Coast Aquarium and Hatfield Marine

Science Center, this motel would be the perfect place to spend a night - easily walk to both aquatic facilities.

The Yaquina Bay bridge is easy to cross on a bike or trike.

NEWPORT TO YACHATS

Newport to Yachats (*pronounced: Ya-hots*) is about as easy and flat as you're going to find along this Oregon Coast Highway, certainly if compared to the capes and heads all up and down the western shore. It's a relaxing interlude prior to Heceta.

Depending on where you camped last night, you may wish to check into South Beach State Park, near MP 143. This state park is on the beach, and is huge. The lands were obtained between 1933 and 1970 with an interest in protecting the area from human encroachment, and also provide public access to the beach. This park covers more than 498 acres, and receives an annual overnight camping population of roughly 145,000 people seeking the Newport experience.

The Newport Municipal Airport comes up on the left shortly after South Beach State Park, at MP 145. We make good time through this relatively uneventful portion of OCH 101 south, with wide shoulder riding and nary a care or fear. The little town of Seal Rock (MP 151) is full of places selling large wooden sculptures and blown glass. About 1600 people call this home. It used to be a vacation destination for the earlier intrepid folks wanting to get in some ocean time. In the 1880s, the Oregon governor even bought land here for occasional visits, and Governor Lord's family still owns a small place in the small village. At fast car speeds, this wide spot in the road comes and goes very quickly, but cycling allows us to enjoy it more fully.

Seal rock is only about 8 miles south of the Yaquina Bay bridge. Notice how wide the shoulders of the highway are here, which on this **Oregon Coast Bike Route** is fairly standard. Up ahead, on the left, will be the wood carving displays and artsy craft shops. Also notice the billboard for Mo's clam chowder restaurants (est. 1946), where you will want to eat at least once. Mo's locations: Cannon Beach, Newport, Otter Rock, Lincoln City, Florence. To learn more online: moschowder.com

From the Mo's website: "When Mohava Marie Niemi, Newport's crusty, big hearted chain smoking mother died in 1992 at the age of 79, she left behind much more than a successful business and a trunk full of colorful anecdotes. Her greatest legacy, perhaps, was the work ethic she instilled in her family, which survives to this day. (photo of Mo, the lovable ol' gal of the sea)

Mo's entry into the business world began in 1940 when she and her father bought the Bay Haven Inn on Newport's salty waterfront. In 1946 they sold the tavern when Mo joined her 'Freddie and Mo's' (a few years later when Freddie became ill, Mo bought her friend out, thus sealing the legacy of Mo's.) The newly divorced mother of two growing sons found it necessary to take a second job, so she became an announcer at local radio station KNPT, where she did a neighborhood talk show, a job she kept until the mid-seventies."

Yum, don't you just want a bowl of Mo's clam chowder?

This is the Alsea Bay bridge, with Waldport on the other side.

Wow, we're really smokin' down the coast road now! Yep, this portion is wide, flat, easy, and fast. I mean, before you know it, MP 155 arrives and is quite obvious with the huge, and recently rebuilt, Alsea Bay bridge. This bridge is easy to ride.

But immediately prior to the crossing is a really nice KOA with cute log cabins that make a perfect place to spend a rainy night, which I did, thus my knowledge. The owners:

134

With the rain coming down, I just didn't feel like pitching my tent at the Beachside State Park 4 miles farther south, so I turned in here, got a cabin, took a hot shower, and kept my trike dry by setting it up on the porch. Sure, I've tent camped in rain before, but the fortuitous arrival of this inviting KOA option got the better of my wet head, so I shelled out a wee bit more money than I would have at Beachside State Park. I enjoyed my stay.

The Waldport welcome sign is just prior to the KOA.

This is the Alsea Bay bridge from the southern side of the river.

A business in Waldport looks like a lighthouse, but it's not.

Waldport (MP 156) is a small town of just over 2,000 residents. Here is how the town promotes itself:

"Moderate year around temperatures rarely dip below freezing. Summer days are in the 70s and the yearly average is 51 degrees, Annual rainfall is about 61 inches. When the tide goes out you can dig clams, rake crabs or comb the beach. Down the road a few miles there is a place out of Lost Horizons - rocks covered with mussels to be gathered, starfish of every hue and color, driftwood that takes on every shape your imagination allows, and a sunset better than any July 4th fireworks display.

"The relative obscurity of Waldport is part of its charm. Here is a quiet city on the beautiful Oregon Coast, offering miles of unspoiled beaches; here is salmon, trout and surf fishing at its best. There is also a nine-hole golf course located in the hills near town. Here is relaxation with a capital R. The beach in the summer, fall, winter and spring is host to beachcombers, joggers, kite fliers, picnickers, horseback riders and many other recreating users. Once known as "the beachcombers paradise," the beaches along the coast here are simply some of the cleanest, nicest and most beautiful in America. While enjoying, feel free to comb for driftwood, glass floats, rocks and shells." - Are you hooked?

This town got its start in the late 1870s, when some adventurers came boating down the Alsea River, and liked it. Waldport is a forest port, and the German word wald (forest) makes it so. The town was laid out in 1879, using the night stars as survey points. Waldport is a burial ground of the Alsi tribe.

Salmon fishing and canning, tree logging, and the dairy businesses have thrived here over the years. There used to be sawmills here. Logging is still active. In 1918, the US Army built a railroad to this town to haul spruce wood for building aircraft. After the war, a logging company bought the railroad, but once they completed cutting the trees in 1935, they left town.

Conde McCullough designed the original Alsea Bay bridge, as he did others on the coast, but it deteriorated by 1986, and was replaced with this new steel bridge in 1991. Conde's designs left a lot to be desired from a hiker or biker's viewpoint, as you'll learn by the time you get to California. He loved cars!

By appearances, it seems unlikely that this bridge architect was a rider of human powered cycles. That pipe indicates his desire to live long was a low priority. It is certain that he never heard of a tricycle like I ride, based on how he had designed several of his bridges, such as the Florence bridge, which has sections that make taking a trike on the sidewalk impossible. His bridges may look eye catching, but if you're not in a car, watch out!

This new Alsea bridge is definitely a **huge** improvement, and you will appreciate its **safe** design when you pedal over it (choice of shoulder **OR** sidewalk)!

Riding south out of Waldport, around the mouth of the Alsea River, 101 heads up a small hill, rounds to the left at the top, and points due south towards California, remaining low and flat along the wide and sandy beach areas. At MP 159, we pass Beachside State park. If you wish to travel quickly, do it now.

Beachside State Park is small, sandwiched between 101 and the sandy beach that leads to its name. There is no buffer here for noise if you choose to camp, but once the night wears on and traffic is of lower volume, all you'll have is the mighty surf lulling you to sleep. The land for this state park was acquired in 1944 to access the large beach at Big Creek, and to preserve the native flora. The first name of the park was Big Creek State Park, but public dissension changed that in 1957 to end any confusion with other locales with a similar name. This camping ground and park area sits on only 16 acres, but the ambiance and views are great. Yearly overnight attendance is a little over 36,000 people.

Not too much farther south, also on the ocean side of the road, is Tillicum Beach Forest Service Campground, one of the few operated by this federal agency on the Oregon Coast. Just past MP 160, we have yet another easy and gorgeous setting where we can duck in off the road for a night of serene oceanside sleeping. There is no shortage of sleeping locales on this ride to California! It's hard to choose each night – more than you need.

If you wanted to do a coastal journey and camp in **each** of the state parks, you'd be on the road for **16 days at least**!

139

The road is wide open and flat south of Waldport – nice shoulders too! Get some action photos riding along this stretch.

To stay at 'em all, you'd have to spend a couple of weeks on this ride, which actually is not a bad idea if you have the time to do it. Many cyclists ride the Oregon Coast in 6-8 days, but two weeks would be incredibly relaxing and a lot of fun, with much to see.

Superman, where are you? I always get a kick out of this naming!

In what seems like nothing flat, probably because the highway is so wonderfully flat, we cover the next 5 miles to what many folks see as Oregon's best kept coastal secret, Yachats – no, it's not pronounced Yak-hats! I made that ugly mistake of oral presentation over twenty years ago when I first arrived in the area as a new resident, and the people I was speaking with simply burst into laughter! Don't let this happen to you!

On the north end of Yachats is the Adobe Resort, one of my favorite dining experiences on this route. Every table looks right out onto the crashing waves. They make a great Cobb salad too!

Yachats (MP 164) is a very liberated little village that celebrates diversity in a big way. This is one town that gives the clear impression of all its citizens communally rolled into one spiritually connected realm. Here, the sense of community pride is evident, and Yachats focuses on lending its support to every citizen's lifestyles, identities, and overall spirit. They say they are a community with an enduring sense of itself. For whatever reasons, this cohesion is more apparent here than anywhere on the coast. Strolling along the waterfront here is as good as it gets!

On the Yachats welcome sign are the words: GEM OF THE OREGON COAST, and this pretty much sums up this little cozy town that sits just north of Cape Perpetua (another good reason to eat at the Green Salmon – need energy to pedal up the cape!). Full time residents number close to 650, and one thing is certain: they all love the ocean. It is here that a 2 mile walk along the "804 Trail" provides some of the most interesting wave crashing on rock action anywhere. The trail begins at Yachats State Park, a day-use area with an ocean viewing platform.

You will also see banners hanging from posts, with the words La De Da Parade printed on them, a July 4 extravaganza. This town has loads of annual summer events.

The Green Salmon café, coffee house, and meeting place is a prime example of community spirit and pride. It's on the left, across 101 from the grocery store. Stop in and meet some local folks, eat some awesome food, and simply relax for a while.

Next, just coast across to the C&K Market to restock your food supplies, which is easy because automobile traffic is light, and the speed limit in town is a strict 25 miles per hour. Then, head over to Yachats State Park for up close views of rocks being pummeled by wave white waters. Everyone loves the view!

The famous "la de da" festival in Yachats is quite a unique event.

The C&K Market is directly across from the Green Salmon.

    A couple of blocks west of the Green Salmon café is the state park, and if you like seagulls, it's your lucky day once again, because there are tons of them here, waiting for you to take their picture (and feed them). Gull portraits are a visitor favorite.

144

You can literally coast your bike to the state park from the Green Salmon café. This is one of the most picturesque and calming places you could hope to spend an hour just hanging out, doing nothing more than watching the mighty ocean waves pound the rocky beach areas. There is no fee. Love it as long as you like!

Yachats State Park is on Second Street, and with a view of the Yachats River as it enters the Pacific Ocean. Migration of gray whales can be viewed right here if you're lucky enough when riding through. The land was acquired from 1928 to 1986. Yachats is an Indian word, and is believed to mean "at the foot of the mountain", which is apropos because this small village of the central coast sits partially on the huge mountain that covers the east side of town, and is bordered on the south by massive Cape Perpetua. As you relax at this park, look up and realize where you will be riding soon: **S**teep **H**illy **I**ntense **T**errain!

This is the viewing platform next to the wooden sign at the state park. This is looking south, as the Yachats River flows to the sea.

In the vicinity of MP 166, just past a bit actually at a roadside turnout (this is easier than a car since you're on a bicycle), look down and you might just spot one of Oregon's privately owned lighthouses. Cape Perpetua shadows it from the south. This is called the Cleft of the Rock lighthouse, and was not originally part of the official Oregon lighthouse system. This lighthouse remains a private residence, formerly owned by Jim Gibbs, who passed away in 2010, and was built by him in 1976. Jim was a former lighthouse keeper of **Terrible Tilly**, the famous and haunted Tillamook Rock lighthouse, and he authored more than 20 books during his lifetime, including one on lighthouses.

Unlike the public lighthouses of Oregon, Cleft of the Rock, and Pelican Bay in Brookings, is not open for visitation. Of course, neither is Terrible Tilly because it sits a mile off shore.

You can actually go inside most of the Oregon Coast lighthouses however, and while on this cycling trip, you should try to visit and tour at least one of them. Volunteers will take you on a personal guided tour, and you'll get to see the glass tower and light at the top. If you do have a GPS unit, search for the coordinates of Latitude: 44.29049 & Longitude: -124.11076 to find Cleft of the Rock. Okay, no more GPS clues folks! I lost my head for a moment. Argh ...

Cleft of the Rock privately owned lighthouse, just south of Yachats, has a great tsunami-safe view of the Pacific Ocean.

Along the Oregon Coast grows an abundance of pampas grass.

WHALE WATCHING SPOKEN HERE

Well, we have been bringing up the topic of whales lately, so now might be as good a time as any to chat a bit about one of Oregon's favorite activities: whale watching! It is so popular, tens of thousands of tourists flock to the coast here yearly to see the whales migrating just off shore. And guess what! Yep, to answer those millions of whale watching questions, Oregon needs a whole lot of whale watching volunteers! If this sounds pretty cool, when you get home from your cycling odyssey, get in touch with the state for details of how you can spend a vacation.

Here are the contact details if you are interested in becoming a happy whale watching volunteer. They need you:

Depoe Bay Whale Center
Oregon Parks and Recreation Department
198 NE 123rd Street
Newport, Oregon 97365

(541)765-3304/3407
fax (541)765-3402
e-mail: whale.watching@state.or.us

Oregon's theme for this delightful activity is "Whale Watching Spoken Here" and when you notice these signs along the way, often at obvious vantage points, pull in to talk with a volunteer. The volunteers go to special training, and when they arrive to staff a particular site, they put up the WWSH sign, and set up a couple of spyglasses on tripods so you can get a closer look. Of course, you can see whales from time to time with just your own two eyeballs at any location, but the officially staffed places may have a higher likelihood of a spotting and watching.

The official state sanctioned whale watching week that you will most likely be around for runs from the last week of August through the first Monday in September. There are two other officially sanctioned times, but one is during the winter (I get to see that one), and the other late March, earlier than most cyclists begin appearing along the coast.

1874 illustration of a gray whale by Charles Scammon

About 200 gray whales opt not to make the entire migration with all their buddies, and they end up hanging out **all summer long** off the salty **coast of Oregon**, Washington, and California. About sixty of these giants seem to prefer Oregon's central coast area so much that serious observers have identified them and taken their photographs. From this group, around 40 swim around between the towns of Lincoln City and Newport, a **25** mile span of **high activity**. Okay, now you know, so if you bring a spyglass with you in your panniers, keep it handy matey!

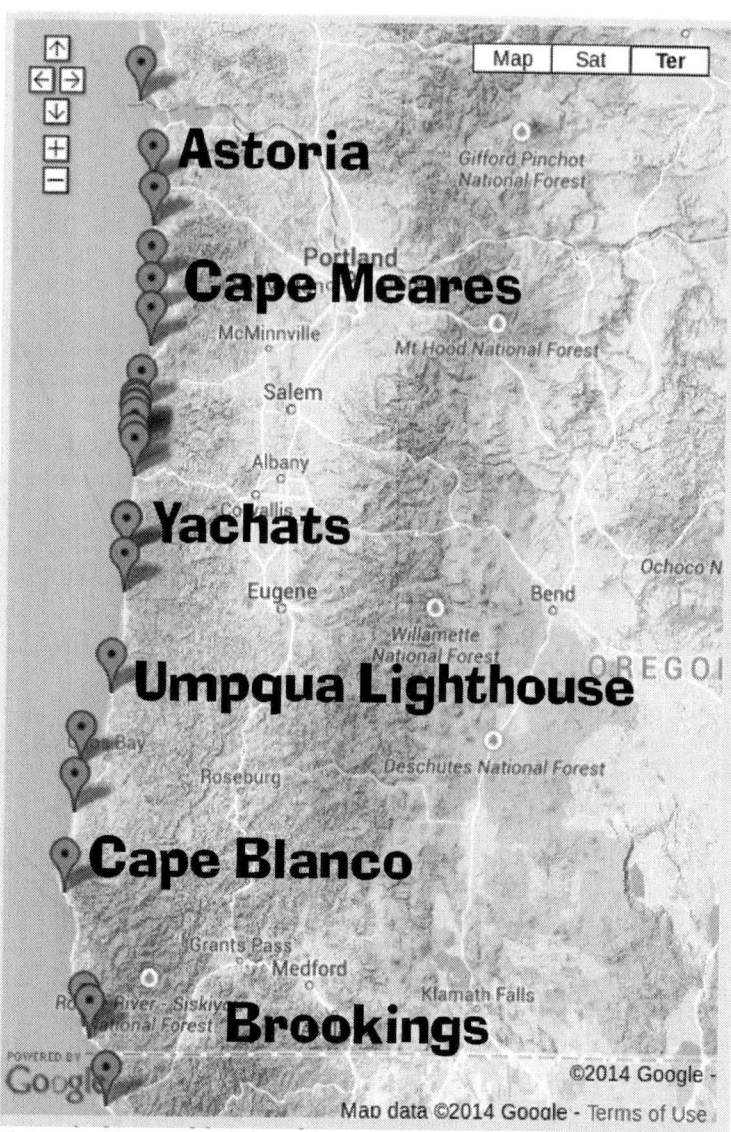

Here are just a few of the places you can watch whales. In reality, it is possible to see them anywhere you can see the ocean. Many folks prefer the high capes and heads, looking down for a more expansive view. It always is fun to keep a lookout westward.

150

The 24 official whale watching sites are (north to south):

Ecola State Park
Neahkahnie Mountain Historic Marker Turnout on Highway 101
Cape Meares State Scenic Viewpoint
Cape Lookout State Park – 2.5 mile hike to site at tip of Cape
Cape Kiwanda
Inn at Spanish Head Lobby on 10th floor
Boiler Bay State Scenic Viewpoint
The Whale Watching Center/Depoe Bay Sea Wall
Rocky Creek State Scenic Viewpoint
Cape Foulweather
Devil's Punchbowl State Natural Area
Yaquina Head Outstanding Natural Area
Don Davis City Park
Cape Perpetua Interpretive Center
Cook's Chasm Turnout
Sea Lion Caves Turnout – Highway 101 turnout south of tunnel
Umpqua Lighthouse, near Umpqua Lighthouse State Park
Shore Acres State Park
Face Rock Wayside State Scenic Viewpoint
Cape Blanco Lighthouse, near Cape Blanco State Park
Battle Rock Wayfinding Point, Port Orford
Cape Sebastian
Cape Ferrelo
Harris Beach State Park, Brookings, Oregon

OREGON COAST GEOLOGY

So, what makes this Oregon Coast look the way it does? Well, to know this, we must delve beneath the surface of things, like the Earth's land masses and the ocean we've been watching along our ride. Remember when we talked a little about tsunamis, those dangerous waves that can destroy a town in a matter of minutes? Well, those are usually initiated by quaking of the Earth, and movement thereof. Little earthquakes can cause little tsunamis, but large earthquakes can really shake things up a bit and cause flooding miles inland along riverways. I actually lived to tell the tale of a tsunami, but it was only 6 inches high, so rarely do I discuss my heroics of the incident.

To learn what the deal is with these forces that generate the deadly tsunamis, I turn now to the Oregon Department of Geology, and will simply toss in a brief quotation from their public offerings:

"Catastrophic hazards are associated with earthquakes and related tsunamis. The eastward-moving Juan de Fuca tectonic plate dives under the westward-moving North American plate just off the Oregon coast at the Cascadia Subduction Zone. Powerful earthquakes up to magnitude 7 can take place in either the North American or the Juan de Fuca plates. The Cascadia Subduction Zone, however, is capable of generating even larger earthquakes — up to magnitude 9.

"These larger earthquakes would occur under the ocean and can cause destructive tsunamis that can strike the coast between 10 and 30 minutes after the earthquake. The geologic record shows that these large Cascadia Subduction Zone earthquakes and accompanying tsunamis occur every 500 years, plus or minus 200 years, with the last one having occurred about 300 years ago.

"Catastrophic hazards on the coast associated with earthquakes include severe ground shaking lasting up to 5 minutes; liquefaction of saturated, unconsolidated soils such as sand or silt; numerous landslides; land subsidence and flooding; and tsunamis."

Okay then, what does this mean to all us pedal pushers out here to have a great time along the beach? Well, to put it quite simply, if you happen to time your journey here just right, and you happen to be tent camping at one of the low-lying state parks, such as Beverly Beach or Sunset Bay, you're history! Both of those state parks, among others, are in little coves, surrounded by mountainous terrain, with one opening that faces the monster Pacific Ocean. If the "event" occurs, and you don't start pedaling right away, you will be slammed with a wall of water, knocked into trees, and swept out to sea, only to be brought back in by the next incoming wave to be slammed around yet again. A waterproof rain fly on your tent will do you no good!

Of course, statistics might suggest that we will not live long enough to see the next "big one" as coastal residents like to call it, so we might as well just forget about all the "what if" scenarios and just live in the present moment! After all, fear is nothing but thought in one's head about some imagined future event, which, in all likelihood, will probably not happen anyway. If you think about all the stuff you worry about all day long, how much of it finally comes to pass? Practically none! I have found that probably 99% of my former worries were groundless, and so I just wasted my present "real" life shaking in my boots about all the bad stuff that might happen to me. Now, I live now.

WHY LIVE IN YACHATS?

Well, to start off, if you can't pronounce the name correctly, then they won't let you live there even if you are wealthy and smart, but if you like Yachats, which you will, are there any compelling reasons to consider it as your final resting place (meaning as you enjoy your senior years)?

This is what the people in Yachats have put together for your consideration. Apparently they are still taking applications for incoming populous because they make it sound so good. Savor this alluring information from their website:

"Almost everyone who visits Yachats recognizes that this is both a unique and special place. When you look at our demographics, we have the oldest population on the Oregon coast. We are also the best educated, according to the most recent census, with many retired educators and professionals living here. Yachats has the highest per capita income on the coast and the second highest in the state of Oregon. Yachats is the gateway to Cape Perpetua and at the north end of what many consider the most beautiful section of the Oregon coast. While it is the physical beauty that initially attracts people to our area, ultimately it is the quality and diversity of the people that encourage many of us to put down roots."

That's enough of that. After all, we left Yachats a couple miles back on our way to Cleft of the Rock lighthouse, so gotta' stop now. Onward to California ...

YACHATS TO FLORENCE

Okay, party's over! No more flat highway for you! Hope you ate very well at the Green Salmon joint, because you're gonna' need all the energy you can muster, and it doesn't take long to get right into the thick of things after pedaling out of Yachats! And if that's not enough to get your attention, besides all the SHIT you'll riding through on the way to MP 191 at the Siuslaw River, there are also two well documented **ghosts** on this portion of the ride, and possibly a third, daughter of one.

But, the **ghosts** can wait until we enter their shadowy domains, because now we must focus on climbing some cliffs! More very tall tops of mountains that frequently live in the low lying cloud cover, high enough where you can't see the summits, where the trees just quietly disappear into the misty lofty realm of nothingness. This is the environment of the sacred headlands!

Just past Gender Creek, which flows into the Pacific south of Gender Drive, the OCH 101 begins its ascent, gentle at first, and you begin your downshifting as necessary. You can't be in a hurry here, just like all the other capes and heads we have already experienced. These sections I refer to as "spin and grin"

because we have no choice but to slow way down, and watch the same tree going by for what seems like an awfully long time. Keep in mind the wise saying: That which does not kill us makes us strong. It's true, and many cyclists eat this stuff up!

This mileage sign greets us south of Yachats. Florence is halfway.

Above is another sign you'll see in short order prior to the real ascent. In Oregon, when you see signs like this, it always means that the state has cast your safety to the wind. Translated, that means government officials are not willing to spend whatever money is necessary to make shoulders along the road because cars don't drive on shoulders, and economic commerce is doing just fine as it is. In other direct words, cars do matter, but human powered humans of any form are not critical to what motivates governing agencies. Lose a cyclist once in a while? Oh well, they were asking for it anyway, riding out there on that deadly road!

If you stayed in Yachats last night, and you are a powerful cyclist, you can make it to Coos Bay today, but what's the rush? There is much incredible scenery between here and there, and speeding through it is not recommended, regardless of how well it may pump up one's image. It is fun though, ha ha.

In the photograph above, take a gander at that tree just behind the bicycle warning sign. Along the coast, especially the headlands, this is the inevitable fate of nearly all trees during their salty life. Winds can and do reach sustained high speeds out here during winter storms, and the battering year after year simply deforms the trees into this slanted posture, where they seem to be pointing to the northeast. During each winter, prevailing extreme winds are southwest, so a snowball in hell stands a better chance of remaining intact than the southwest sides of trees.

My first year in Florence saw one winter storm with winds reaching a whopping 119 MPH, blowing down hundreds of trees in town! One man was killed when a tree fell on his truck. This is serious stuff! Weird trees tell the tale.

Just think of all the things attempting to do you in here. It's enough to make a cyclist think twice about doing this ride, or, for some folks, enough to motivate them even more to come here on their bicycle. We have earthquakes, tsunamis, hurricane force winds, tight curvy blind shoulderless roads on steep uphills, cars seeking targets, you name it. And if none of that gets you, a heart attack on the capes and heads will. Yep, you better well be in damn good physical condition if you hope to finish this 383 mile (616 kilometer) ride that has a total rise and fall of nearly 16,000 feet (4900 meters). This isn't a cake walk by any means!

The 26 miles separating Yachats from Florence are considered the most hazardous on the entire coastal route by some cyclists due to the concentration of very tight, very blind, very narrow roadway, which frequently has little or no shoulder for cyclists. Also, due to the heavy forested landscape, much of all this is in deep shade, making it dark even on sunny days. Motorists' eyes constantly must readjust to conditions. This is simply the reality here, but all that being said, I have never found these factors to cause me to think I'm going to get killed. From the view folks in cars have, it seems like a suicide mission to ride this route over the capes, but from the stance of cyclists, reality reveals that cars always seem to pass on by without incident. After all, with all these bright signs, all brilliant yellow these days, warning them, they don't want to risk all their life savings over a potential lawsuit by hitting a cyclist.

Just ride this section of road like you would any other and you will be fine. Think about this: you can ride in sheer panic the whole way, missing all the great views, and still come out alive on the other side, OR, you can ride with nary a care in the world, love every minute of these awesome views, and, like the one who was worried sick, also come out the other side to tell the tale. Worry, caused by fear-induced thoughts in your head about potential future events, will NOT make you any safer or less safe.

The road is now getting steeper at this sign telling you about entering the Cape Perpetua Scenic Area in the Siuslaw National Forest. This first headland (of two) is breathtaking. Enjoy it!

The word Siuslaw that you will notice on many things in and around the Florence area is taken from the name of a tribal group of first inhabitants of the land. The Siuslaw National Forest is quite large, and extends inland across the Coast Range. Like

Yachats, this Siuslaw also is in need of some pronunciation instruction. So, here I will attempt to indicate how to say it out loud, and also in your head when you read it to yourself: **sigh-Ooh-slaw**, with the emphasis on the Ooh part, which sounds like the double "o" in the word food. Sigh is like when we let out a relaxed tone (making it over the cape unharmed perhaps), and slaw is like what you eat at a restaurant for lunch or dinner.

Actually, this ride up and over this mountainous terrain north of Florence isn't just Cape Perpetua alone. Once over the cape, there is a quite lengthy segment that opens up along the ocean once again, with wide shoulders, straight road, and easy pedaling, and then south of that, we head back up in elevation once again on our ascent of Heceta Head, where the most photographed lighthouse in the United States is loftily perched. This is the Heceta Head lighthouse, and yes, it has a **ghost** that roams the keeper's old house. More on that shortly! I think the reason folks get spooked about this Yachats to Florence stretch is because there stand headlands going into and out of it, thereby giving the impression that the whole thing is risky business. Hey, the middle is many miles of gorgeous riding, and nothing to fear!

I'm a writer, and writers are always juggling how to present things to a vast audience of people, some of whom are seasoned pros riding cross country and never worry about things, and some of whom are newcomers who truly are scared about this journey they really want to take. Thus, on the one hand, it may seem like I'm being too dramatic about the dangers, but neophytes want to know this stuff, and on the other hand it may seem like I'm being too nonchalant about it all. Since I do not know your level of experience, nor your susceptibility to fear, it is impossible to gauge accurately how you will perceive this trip. We are all different. I have seen folks righteously horrified about riding over the Coos Bay bridge, for example, and others think nothing of it. So, this is where a writer is hopelessly stuck, trying to strike a balance with fear and reality that will present an accurate picture of it all. Accuracy will reveal itself when you ride this coastline – it's all relative, in your head – accurate for you!

Before I rode this route, I was worried about this car/bike safety issue, but having had no negative incidents, I have evolved to a point of inner peace. It's either that, or don't ride anymore!

You can see that shoulders on the way up to the summit of this Cape Perpetua road are not sufficient to contain a cyclist, and at places, there is no shoulder at all. This is why I recommend to you that wearing bright yellow garments, and having bright yellow panniers are wise choices. I also have a flag on the back of the trike, along with high visibility safety triangles so I "pop" out of the shadows in the eyes of the car drivers. Yes, this all works!

Yachats behind us, from high on Cape Perpetua, now disappears.

This is looking south towards Heceta Head. The lighthouse is down there near the pointed rock sticking up from the ocean, on the south side of the headland. Between here and there, the road eases up with leisurely riding even for the more timid cyclists. Many people call this Oregon's most scenic coastline of all.

Just past the apex of the cape, as you begin heading down to the popular Cape Perpetua Visitor's Center, you'll pass a small concessionaire stand on the right, at Devil's Churn, which sells coffee. Then down from there around the corner is the visitor's center if you wish to learn about the area, and up a small rise you come to the huge parking area for the Spouting Horn and Thor's Well, two really cool natural holes you are definitely going to want to see! Everyone stops here, and so will you!

Watch for the following waysides to gauge your progress over the tops of these two rather large hills: Lincoln/Lane county line (MP 167), Neptune State Scenic Viewpoint (MP 168), Strawberry Hill State Park (MP 169), Bob Creek (MP 170), Stonefield Beach State Park (MP 171), Rock Creek Campground (small USFS MP 174), Muriel Ponsler State Park (MP 175), and then Carl Washburn State Park next door.

162

the original buggy road around Cape Perpetua

At the cape's highest summit point, this is one of the photos on the placard that explains the rough times of making a roadway.

This sign is on your left after flying down the hill from 101's summit, and passing the side road to the cape's highest point.

Heceta Head from Cape Perpetua

This photo was taken at the summit of the cape, accessible on a paved, but very steep, side road just prior to the visitor's center.

The building midway on the left is the visitor's center. The Spouting Horn is visible near upper right corner of photograph.

There is a hiking trail to the top of the cape, narrow and steep. There is also a paved road suitable for an extremely fit bicyclist.

This hole sucks in the ocean. It is very dangerous. It's at the same turnout for the Spouting Horn, past the Perpetua visitor's center.

the Spouting Horn

Around the curve south of the Cape Perpetua Visitor Center is a large parking area, where you can stop to see the Spouting Horn.

A lone crow sits atop Thor's Well, watching the action.

Partway between Cape Perpetua and Heceta Head is the modern Big Creek bridge. These miles are open, scenic, and memorable!

Carl Washburne State Park (MP 176) was named after the Eugene, Oregon Highway Commissioner of the same name, who served from 1932 to 1935. He was also a successful businessman in the inland Willamette Valley. This park's land was a gift from the Washburne estate in 1962. Washburne State Park is just over 1,000 acres, and it receives a yearly overnight population of more than 34,000 campers. The ocean is right across the highway, so if you camp here, you can walk the beach before your hot shower and bedding down. This campground is about 9 miles south of Cape Perpetua. I recommend it.

The above photo is a northward view from a hiking trail that originates at the lighthouse and heads north up to the top of Heceta Head. This is looking north to Cape Perpetua, which you see as the distant headland. From Cape Perpetua, you can see Yachats, and from Heceta Head, you can see Florence, and from either, you can see the other headland. These views pretty much encompass the Yachats to Florence stretch of OCH 101.

About a mile after leaving Carl's campground, the road curves sharply right and heads down a hill into a hairpin left hand turn, and here we find Heceta Head lighthouse. It sits 205 feet above sea level, and is 56 feet tall. Apparently, it is the most photographed lighthouse around. The beam is the most powerful of the Oregon lighthouses, and can be seen by mariners 21 miles distant on the ocean. Once every 10 seconds the beam is cast seaward, but it's not just one beam. When you watch it at night, you observe it is multiple beams that rotate, and it takes the 10 seconds for the next beam in line to reach your eyes. (MP 178)

Construction was begun in 1892, but it was slowed by the utter seclusion of this seaside location. If weather and water cooperated, the supplies were brought here by ship, if not, they were hauled on a wagon from the town of Florence, 13 miles south, which could take about 5 hours. This lighthouse is 13 miles north of Florence, and 13 miles south of Yachats. It was completed in 1897, at a cost of $80,000. In 1932, the coast road was finished to Yachats, and reaching the lighthouse was easier.

From the bridge that leads into the Cape Creek tunnel, this view of the lighthouse is seen. If you lift your bike up onto the sidewalk at the end of the bridge where you push the button for the flashing tunnel lights, you can walk back to here for this photo. There is a visitor parking area down below the highway.

Now, if you're planning on visiting this lighthouse, do so in the daytime, because ... yes, it's indeed very **haunted** on this patch of land. But you know what's totally cool about this **ghost** story? The old house for the lightkeeper has been made into a bed and breakfast, so, you can spend the night there if you make your reservations at least 3 months in advance. If you like **ghosts**, I mean REALLY like them, this opportunity is perfect to finally see one personally! Arrive in the area on your bike a day early.

Camp at Carl Washburne State Park the nigh prior, or spend the night in a Yachats motel. Get to the lighthouse by check-in time, sit on the deck overlooking the ocean, eat a grand dinner, and prepare to experience the paranormal like few ever have the chance to do! This is the real deal, and keeps on giving.

This location was named after Bruno de Heceta y Dudagoitia, who discovered it in 1755, at least from a "white" man's perspective, as the first inhabitant tribal people had predated him by a very long time. I may as well explain how to pronounce this Spaniard's name, according to everyone who lives around here anyway. It is NOT heck-a-ta, as one might initially say. It is pronounced heh-See-tah. Okay, now you are saying it correctly in your head as you read about it on these pages. If you are curious about why Bruno de Heceta y Dudagoitia was here in the first place, I have a little story about him shortly.

Let's first talk a moment or two about Rue, the resident **apparition** you will meet first-hand if you spend the night. Stories can vary when one talks to people about **ghosts**, usually because no one living knew the **spirit** personally prior to its death. So here is trike hobo's rendition, for whatever it's worth:

In the 1890s, Rue was married to the assistant keeper of the light, and lived on the grounds with her husband and daughter. One tragic day, their daughter went missing while playing, and it was concluded that she had most likely drowned and been swept out to sea. Rue, understandably, went into a state of depression, and eventually became so distraught that she committed suicide here. Even with her passing though, she never has stopped looking for her daughter. Others say the daughter's body was found and buried on the grounds, and Rue remains in residence simply to be with her. Either way, Rue is still here. And yes, a little girl's grave is reportedly on these very premises!

Reports of **Rue's presence** persist to this day, and by reputable folks who have nothing to gain from spreading paranormal stories. In fact, they have everything to lose because some might think them mad. One typical story comes from the early 1970s, when guests were over having dinner with the keeper and his family. While relaxing in the sitting room after dining, a **blood curdling** scream was heard, and they all tell that is seemed to come from the <u>center</u> of the room, where they were all facing!

The two cats instantly jumped in the air and ran. The keeper got up to investigate, and briefly saw a long **white skirt** moving across the hall, while also hearing the air movement a skirt would make if moving rapidly. The **image** moved through a locked door without opening it. A few moments later, while putting away dishes in the kitchen, the wife saw this same apparition glide through another door – that was the end of those dishes she had in her hands! **It** was also seen gliding up the very dark stairway moments later, just gliding – no stepping.

At another time, a maintenance worker was cleaning windows and saw a reflection in the glass. He abruptly turned around, only to see a **lady in a white skirt** advancing on him. He didn't wait around to learn any more, and refused to ever enter the attic again. However, once when he was cleaning the attic window form the outside (he needed the job), he again was confronted with **Rue** staring at him from inside. In his haste to get down the ladder, he accidentally broke a window pane. This was enough – the man resigned his position. But later that night, others said they heard brushing noises from upstairs. The next morning, when they went up to the attic (no one would go at night anymore), they saw the broken window pane glass had been swept into a tidy little pile for its removal. It is said that Rue was a known neat-nick, and thus this all makes perfect sense. Rue also has earned the moniker **Gray Lady**, from folks reporting that her appearance is usually a **smoky gray mist**.

I have spent a couple of evenings in this sitting room during the Christmas season when the keeper's house is open to the public, but in the presence of probably at least two dozen other people. It's crowded inside the house because it has typical small Victorian styled rooms. You know why all the locals come up to the house these nights? Well, to be witness to Rue!

To make your reservations, visit hecetalighthouse.com, or call 1-866-547-3696, which will ring you through to Yachats, where they handle the visitor bookings. The current keepers are Michelle Korgan and Steven Bursey. You can even get gift certificates to share the fun! Rue may spook you, but she is not malicious at all, just still missing her daughter, and wanting to keep the keeper's house tidy. Oh, one more thing ... she used to ride a bicycle. Over and out ...

Above is the light keeper's home at Heceta Head, which sits perched atop the Cape Creek River that enters the ocean here. The views from the bench out front are awesome, and it's fun to imagine this being one's own personal home. Rue lives here.

The Cape Creek tunnel is in the trees at the far end of the bridge.

The 714 foot Cape Creek tunnel was built in 1932. The interior lighting is VERY bright, and cyclists show up very well. Relax!

This bicyclist was given plenty of room by the trucker. Easy!

FLEAS ON A DOG

I am a flea, and I live in a forest of fur on a dog. Of course, I have no knowledge of what a dog even is (*Dog reversed is God*), nor do I understand its fur. All I know is that my domain is large and its environment allows me to live free. I have explored far and wide this realm of mine, and then one day, I see a flea just like me, and realize there are others! I have to share?

Not wishing to share my domain, I stand up on my hind legs and proclaim officially all this vast fur as exclusively mine. I make the claim, and no one rises up to dispute it. I am content with my property. I now own the fur in which I live.

Then one day, another flea approaches me and lets me know there are some new fleas setting up home on the underside of the dog. How can they do this, I wonder? Don't they know I have claimed this dog as my own? They are encroaching. I better travel down there and make sure my claims are honored! So, I set out to explore the region on the other side, and make sure any unauthorized fleas leave immediately.

Well, of course, this silly little story is silly, right? Okay, so it is, but it illustrates precisely what goes on with humans, and sets the stage for the naming of the Heceta Head lighthouse, and all other locales with Heceta in their name! Fleas at least know how to share. We could learn a thing or two.

In the late 1490s, Spain formally announced to the world that it had exclusive right to colonize darn near all of the western hemisphere of Planet Earth (the nerve of those fleas)! This included the north coast regions we are currently pedaling our cycles on in this book. But that was not enough. In 1513, Vasco Núñez de Balboa sailed out to Panama, and then claimed the entire Pacific Ocean belonged to Spain, as well as all the lands that touched it! Well, that sealed it! Spain had conquered an entire planet, or pretty close, at least. They were content with this.

But then, word filtered in to the Spanish crown that some other bold fleas had begun to settle on Spanish fur in what we call the Pacific Northwest. How dare them! So, Spain sent official ships over there to stop this unauthorized encroachment, one of which was commanded by intrepid explorer Bruno de Heceta y Dudagoitia, sailing the Santiago, along with a second ship. They were charged with making sure those evil British and Russian fleas got the hell out of Spanish fur holdings.

If we had been here on bikes and trikes back then, we would have seen these two ships scurrying around out there in the water to find trespassers just like us, and when they did find settlements, they reasserted the Spanish "right" to this dog and all its vast fur. Bruno de Heceta y Dudagoitia also sailed past the Clatsop Spit, thinking the Columbia was a great waterway connecting to another ocean, but the current kept him out. So, this Heceta guy fell into the history of coastal Oregon!

Perhaps not quite too surprising, this cycle of "all mine" came around again in 1888, when Europeans from eastern America were the latest folks who stumbled upon Heceta Head and officially proclaimed 164 acres as their own patch of private fur. Then, the US government got into the act and gave the okay to build a lighthouse. The intrepid explorer Bruno de Heceta y Dudagoitia would have been furious! How dare them!

Yours truly, with trike, at the Heceta Head lighthouse overlook.

Just past that photo of me on the wall is this well-known attraction visited annually by untold thousands of coastal visitors. Sea Lion Caves (MP 179), is a privately owned wildlife preserve, and the year-round home of the famous Stellar sea lion. Visit sealioncaves.com for more information.

South of Sea Lion Caves is this vista over the sand lands of the south, where Florence is located, and this ride's half-way point.

MP 183 is Alder Dune, and MP 185 is Sutton, north of Florence.

Not far north of the town limit is a woodcarver at **Mystic Woods** who makes all kinds of imaginary figurines from cedar. You will see this wizard if it is not sold by the time you arrive. If it has been sold, he will probably make another one, because these wizards are quite popular. That's a glass float in his hand.

Having just passed a couple of nice campgrounds, we are now entering Florence, where the prized half-way marker for the **Oregon Coast Bike Route** is found. We have two outstanding campground options here, as well as motels and laundries.

Shoulders are wide and flat. Fred Meyer superstore is coming up.

184

The vast majority of cyclists pedaling the Oregon Coast stay at Jessie M. Honeyman Memorial State Park, with its hot showers and private hiker/biker camp area. It is about 3 miles south of Florence. The **Port of Siuslaw** however has a **laundry** also, which means you can wash your clothes **while** you camp at their outstanding hiker/biker area! Not only that, but this is Old Towne, and you can **walk** the boardwalk and **dine** at the eateries.

FLORENCE, OREGON HISTORY SUMMARY

1876: First homesteaders were welcomed by Siuslaw Indians, who already lived here. Early homesteaders came by ship to Coos Bay or Gardiner, and then by overland stage along the beach to what eventually became the town of Florence. The stage vehicle had wide steel tires, and was pulled by a team of four horses, hitched side by side, so no horse would step in the wake of the one ahead, thereby allowing team to pull through quicksand.

1878: The town of Florence was formally established. Common local belief is the name came from a ship called the Florence, which shipwrecked attempting to enter the Siuslaw River. A large wooden sign from the Florence was salvaged, and found its way onto a business in town, and the name stuck. The Florence sank off shore in 1875.

1905: Florence was flourishing as a town, with canned salmon and lumber the two major exports that allowed the town to exist in the early days. Most exports were sent by ship to San Francisco, and goods from there were imported into Florence on return voyages.

1910: Huge fire destroyed much of town (what is now called Old Town), where today's Mo's Restaurant and ICM Restaurant stand.

1919: Canning of salmon ceased as an export business. Lumber continued as major export.

1930s: Coast highway was completed, with the Siuslaw River bridge now allowing automobile traffic to arrive and depart. Ferry was no longer needed, thus dismantled.

GHOST SHIPS (some of the unlucky ones that crashed here):

1875: Florence shipwrecked off shore – reason for town's name
1902: Nettie Somberg
1903: Ocean Spray
1905: Bella
1912: Wilhelmena
1913: Anvil
1913: Oakland
1960: Humbolt Woodsman (barge leaving harbor, ran aground)

IS IT HALF-TIME YET?

Everyone likes to keep track of things to a certain extent, and I suppose that for cyclists who are on a time schedule for this trip, knowing how one is progressing from Washington to California might be important. I like to keep a mental image of where I am too, but just for the fun of it, or perhaps for the challenge of keeping my head active.

Have you ever wondered where the precise half way mark is on this **Oregon Coast Bike Route**? Well, of course, how does one go about determining this magical place of middleness? The short answer is that it can't be figured out by those not using GPS, but for all you satellite aficionados, it's probably easy. But alas, I have opted to just ride like the old days, and have no sophisticated tracking devices on my trike other than my human brain. Here is my discussion of this half way topic:

There are 363 milepost markers along the Oregon Coast, with the first one being a mile south of the Washington state line, over the Columbia River, and the final one being at the California state line. The last southern number is 363, so if we divide 363 by 2, to discover the half way point, we arrive at MP 181 (no tenths allowed). Where is this marker located? MP 181 appears in the vicinity of Southview Estates, which is a little more than 7 miles prior to entering the coastal town of Florence. Initially, this would seem like what we seek, but there's an MP glitch at Bandon.

And there's even more to consider here! Yes, here is what the state of Oregon officially says in its *Oregon Coast Bicycle Route Map*: "The total length of the signed bike route is 370 miles (595 km). It can be lengthened to 380 miles (610 km) by taking the alternate Three Capes Scenic Route."

This book insists on taking the Three Capes Scenic Route, as well as the Seven Devils scenic diversion, the Otter Crest Loop bypass, and the Cape Blanco diversion. So, if we do the 380 mile number, we cannot use milepost markers as our half way guide. We must recalculate to discover the magical place that signals we only have that much again to pedal. Now, when we divide 380 by 2, we arrive at 190. Is that precise to a gnat's eyebrow hair? Probably not, but it's good enough for this hobo trike trekker, so I shall honor this place in this official guidebook.

MP 190 is a few yards past Abby's Pizza, which is across the highway. Each person may well have a different view of this monumental question – such is life! It could be just north of town or maybe just south, but this MP is easy to find and justify.

The midpoint of the **Oregon Coast Bike Route** as suggested in this book is MP 190, or at least somewhere in the neighborhood.

Just around this curve is where Highway 126 takes off eastward over the Coast Range for Eugene, Oregon, the state's second largest city. Hwy 126 is what many cyclists ride if they are going to New York or points east, or coming from there. The **bicycle shop** is on the NW corner of Highway 101 and 8th Street:

Stopping for a big bowl of steamy clam chowder at Mo's is a must-do requirement for all bikers and trikers. There are several of these on the coast of Oregon, so you have an option of which one you visit, or, if you are focused on trying every Mo's, then this is the Florence version, right on the Siuslaw River at the dock in Old Towne! Abby's or Mo's? It's your call.

The dock next to Port of Siuslaw campground is picturesque.

Some big ships dock here at Old Towne. Explore a little.

OREGON COAST CYCLING GHOST

During our half-time intermission, I'll introduce one final **ghost**. Well, this fellow is not quite a **ghost**, but he seems so. They say old cyclists never die, they just fade away, and this eternally wandering soul may be caught somehow in the fading phase, wafting back and forth perpetually. You may see him however!

The Oregon Coast Cycling Ghost is often found hanging out around the Siuslaw River Coffee Roasters, in Old Towne, just below the bridge at the south end of town. During my 2013 overland trike journey down the Pacific Coast to Morro Bay, I caught up to the elusive Oregon Coast Cycling Ghost while he was heading out to parts unknown. This was a rare occurrence indeed due to his fading out completely and then reappearing. I have come to believe he has no control over his apparent destiny, disappearing not according to any wish of his own, but based on some supernatural plan out of his control.

I first saw what appeared to be a normal coastal rider up ahead about a quarter mile. By the time I got close enough to capture the following photograph, the rider began quickly fading out, and I knew then who I was following! My heart raced ...

I pedaled quickly to try to talk with him, but by the time I pulled up alongside at MP 197, there was no one there to talk to – gone! His clothing consists of black jersey material, and he wears a black cap, so when he begins fading, it happens fast. He rides many different types of bikes, but he's always on the road.

Your best chance to see the Oregon Coast Cycling Ghost is to visit the Siuslaw River Coffee Roasters. It is not uncommon to find him there in the afternoons, surrounded by other cycle tourists lucky enough to see him fully visible. If he is visible, and spots you touring, he usually will approach you to talk all about your trip and bike. He is also known to **frequent the bike shop**!

When he is in his fully visible state, he can talk and act like any normal cyclist, but once the elusive fading phase begins, all such ability disappears. The fade-out happens quickly, and I suspect he has some sense of when it's coming, because he often heads off on his bike. The chap is really friendly, not at all a trouble making **ghost** He loves to share all things associated with bicycle touring, and will provide you plenty of useful advice and tips about not only Florence, but cycling the route from Canada to Mexico, which he seems to favor. No one is aware of why this unique **ghost** prefers the west coast, but one thing is certain: if you can find him, he makes for one hell of a great conversation!

FLORENCE TO NORTH BEND

This stretch of coast opens up compared to what we have been riding on the northern coast, as it parallels the Oregon Dunes National Recreation Area, which spans from Florence to the north spit jetty at the entrance to Coos Bay. Coos Bay is an inland bay, but has a long waterway inlet to arrive at it by boat. Spanning the bay on OCH 101 is the infamous Coos Bay bridge, known technically as Conde McCullough Memorial bridge.

Prior to this giant bridge, which is 2,082 feet longer than the Yaquina Bay bridge we crossed in Newport a few days ago, we also ride over a draw bridge at Reedsport, and get to visit another lighthouse in Winchester Bay. Florence to North Bend is a pleasant ride with wide shoulders, no tunnels, and devoid of any daunting capes or heads. For fit cyclists, this is a distance that can easily be accomplished in one day.

The Oregon Dunes National Recreation Area is about 40 miles long, formed over time by wind, water, and the perpetual forces of the natural world. Some of the dunes exceed 500 feet in height! They are the largest expanse of coastal dunes in North America, and you will have opportunities to view them on this part of the coast highway. Many tens of thousands of "duners" visit these immense sand landforms every year, landforms that are often changing shape due to the wind. Duners consist of people who use dune buggies, motorcycles, and small qaudmobiles to recreate and explore the seemingly endless nooks and crannies of sand. On weekends and holidays, traffic is heavy to the dunes.

We exit Florence on the Siuslaw River bridge, which is slightly uphill going south. This bridge is much smaller than the Yaquina Bay bridge at Newport, but the car lane must be ridden due to Conde's poor architectural design choices for humans.

The Siuslaw River bridge as viewed from Old Towne, looking west. The center portion is a draw bridge, where you see the mobile home driving. After sunset, excellent photos can be taken!

Here is Old Towne Florence at night, when all the action starts. You can walk to the Port of Siuslaw campground from here.

Leaving the Port of Siuslaw campground at sunrise provides this gorgeous view from the Siuslaw River bridge when pedaling out.

**The North Coast lies behind us!
The South Coast lies before us!**

Time for the

OFFICIAL INTERMISSION

Here now is the

**HALF-WAY PHOTO GALLERY
OF
OREGON COAST BIKE ROUTE
CYCLISTS**

Understand their adventures
by discovering your own!

GO HAVE A CLIF BAR

Then come back ready for more!

You'll pass MP 191 while crossing the Siuslaw River bridge, and then gear down to climb the hill on the other side. At the top of the hill is the road to the south jetty, which puts you right on the beach, but it's downhill and a couple miles to the ocean, so you may opt not to take it. Shortly after MP 193 we arrive at Jessie M. Honeyman Memorial State Park, which is the big favorite for most cyclists for spending the night in their tents. This is an alternative to the Port of Siuslaw camp area in Old Towne – both have showers, but Honeyman has no laundry, nor does it offer Old Towne literally within walking distance from the tent. Choices! My recommendation is the Port of Siusalaw.

Jessie M. Honeyman Memorial State Park covers 515 acres, and receives more than 147,000 overnight campers each year, many of whom are bikers who stay in the hiker/biker camp area. This state park is in a thick gigantic evergreen forest, with massive trees the view at every campsite. The beach is a long hike through deep sand from here, but it's possible for motivated people. This land was purchased from private owners between 1930 and 1936, and the park was named after the Portland woman who strongly advocated for roadside beauty on the Oregon Coast. She used to guide Samuel Boardman, who was the first Oregon State Parks superintendent, around this region.

Cleowox Lake borders the park on the north, and can be walked to after pitching your tent. The old stone bathhouse at the lake was built in the 1930s by the Civilian Conservation Corps.

The southern coast seems more wild and open, in that there are fewer towns along the route, and much of the scenery has remained unchanged since days of yore. If you are interested in "making time" down to California, the more primitive southern portion of this ride will allow you to do so. A fit rider can easily hit the California state line three days out from Florence. Towns are farther apart in the south. In this half is the highest bridge.

There are campground options along the way however, in addition to the state parks where most cyclists opt to stay at night. Just prior to MP 199, is Carter Lake campground, which is off the highway on an old paved road. A small lake here remains warm enough in the summer months for swimming, and a trail through the tiny forest leads to the beach and ocean. There are also occasional overlooks to view the Oregon Dunes National Recreation Area from time to time, one of the first coming up shortly prior to MP 210. A short trail leads to the viewing area, where an expanse of ocean and dunes can be seen. Tahkenitch Campground is a nice spot to stop for a snack on the left side of the road in the vicinity of MP 203. It sits on the west shore of Tahkenitch Lake, surrounded by forest. Like Carter Lake camp area, this is not developed with showers or some of the other amenities sought by bicyclists on a tour.

Soon, we climb Gardiner Hill, rather long, but easy, prior to summiting and plunging down the south face into the small old town of Gardiner. Most of 101 is plenty wide in this section.

Matt Jensen rests at the top of Gardiner Hill, north of the town.

You'll know when you reach the top of Gardiner Hill, as you can see open vistas of clear-cut forests to the right, distant ocean, and a highway that falls away down the mountain for the next mile. Get ready for your high speed coast down into the town of Gardiner, one of the river villages that has definitely seen better days. If you choose not to use your brakes on this nearly straight descent, which is not really necessary due to the lack of curves, you will very quickly reach speeds in excess of 45 miles per hour. There is a now defunct paper mill at the bottom.

MP 209 marks your short bout of pedal pushing through this bygone town, and it is less than 2 miles to the next draw bridge, past the Smith River, and into Reedsport, an old logging town that has been not so engaged in logging as it used to be years ago. The Smith River bridge is recent construction, very wide, and has a super wide cycling lane. Oh, it's also just about flat, so no need to slow down here. Time for lunch!

Reedsport is a rural town, with peaceful easy streets, and even a big Safeway supermarket if you need to resupply your panniers. There is a great Mexican restaurant just past the first signal on the right if you like Mexican food. You should be here shortly prior to lunch time, perfect timing for chips and salsa. The road is easy riding to the Umpqua Lighthouse, then another hill.

The town of Reedsport (MP 211) sits on the pretty banks of the Umpqua River, and is near the confluence of three rivers: the Umpqua, Smith, and Scholfield. The Umpqua River is the largest river in between the Columbia, which we left several days ago at Clatsop Spit, and the Sacramento, down towards central California. Not too far back, at MP 198, we entered Douglas County, and up ahead at MP 220, we shall leave Douglas County, and right here in the middle sits Reedsport. From a coastal standpoint, Douglas County is sparsely populated, but we'll be seeing one more town prior to departing it.

Reedsport, a coastal town that sits inland, has two large markets.

In Reedsport, as also in Florence, Waldport, Newport, Lincoln City, and Tillamook, there is a highway that allows access to the coast from inland regions of the highly populated Willamette Valley. In that valley are found cities like Eugene, Salem, and Portland. Highway 38 is the one that leads inland from Reedsport, and if you travel a little more than 3 miles on

38, you'll see the Dean Creek Elk Viewing Area, which supports a large population of Roosevelt elk (nearly always here).

It is a very rare sight to see two bulls fighting at Dean Creek.

Here comes the Reedsport draw bridge that crosses the Umpqua River into Reedsport. Shoulders are super wide. Riding is easy.

This is the Reedsport draw bridge. It is short, level, and easy.

After our Mexican lunch in Reedsport at the Atzlan restaurant, we leisurely pedal a couple or three more miles into Winchester Bay (MP 215), a really quaint little fishing village that also boasts plenty of busy ATV activity on the dunes, tours of the famous Umpqua Lighthouse, and the catching of crabs (the kind you eat). Winchester Bay calls itself the Crab Capital of the World. Smack dab in the middle of town is Salmon Harbor. The Umpqua River, which passes through Reedsport, flows into the Pacific Ocean here at Winchester Bay.

If you wish to see Umpqua Lighthouse, or if you wish to camp at Umpqua Lighthouse State Park, you have to make a minor decision here in Winchester Bay. You can continue up the long 101 hill immediately south of town, turning right at the sign for the lighthouse, or, you can take Salmon Harbor Drive through town, and then turn left in a mile at Lighthouse Road to come in the other way. Salmon Harbor Drive to Lighthouse Road is pretty and scenic, and I recommend it for the awesome ocean vistas!

Umpqua Lighthouse State Park is a small one, at just over 362 acres, with an average annual overnight attendance of slightly more than 28,000 people. The actual camping area is small, and often filled up with campers, but like all Oregon State Parks, there is a hiker/biker area and you can never be turned away! You can stay at any state park, during the absolute heaviest times of the summer touring season, no matter what time you arrive! **Bikers are guaranteed a camping spot on the coast.**

Above: Umpqua River, Reedsport. Below: Winchester Bay ships.

Quite a bit of this state park was given to the state by Douglas County, and they acquired additional land from the US government and private owners. Development of park facilities was begun in the 1930s by the Civilian Conservation Corps at little Lake Marie (a **great** swimming lake, by the way). By the late 1950s, the current camping area was added.

The Umpqua lighthouse was erected in 1857 to mark the entry point of the Umpqua River for boat traffic. This was the first lighthouse on the Oregon Coast. But bad things happened. Within 6 years, the lighthouse was pretty much done-in by the weather. The Oregon lighthouse builders learned not to build the lighthouses on a sandy spit of unstable land.

Oregon's second lighthouse was built at Cape Arago. In 1888, the Lighthouse Board finally gave the okay for a second lighthouse at the mouth of the Umpqua River, but this one was constructed on real ground on a hill, guaranteeing that it would not meet a similar fate of the first house. In December 1894, the light from the new second lighthouse began to shine seaward to announce the Umpqua River to all ocean going ships.

The US Coast Guard has a station that sits immediately next to this structure. If you choose to camp at this state park, I recommend walking here from your tent to see the sunset if it is a clear evening. If you like to swim, Lake Marie is perfect.

Here is a sunset I captured, across from the Umpqua lighthouse.

The campground sits on the east shore of Lake Marie (left side).

The state park campground is to the left of this sign, on Lighthouse Road, which is the loop road from Winchester Bay.

This vista is at the top of the hill on 101, past the lighthouse area.

From Winchester Bay, it's about 20 miles south to North Bend, where the gigantic bridge spanning a bay called Coos is located. We are still paralleling the Oregon Dunes National Recreation Area as we pass Clear Lake on our left, and then arrive at William M. Tugman State Park just north of the little town of Lakeside (MP 222). Tugman State Park pops up just past MP 221 a half mile, and is situated in lovely forest along 101.

Eel Lake was becoming clogged with logging debris, and as a means to protect public access to the lake, the state acquired this land from the Oregon State Game Commission and private owners. Prior to transfer of ownership, the Commission cleaned out all the logging mess from the otherwise pristine coastal lake. The name of a prominent fellow in the newspaper business was assigned to this park, because he headed a committee that advocated for state park development in the 1950s.

Over 560 acres make up Tugman State Park with great camping and hot showers, and nearly 40,000 people camp here every year. As you are learning, there are more state parks on this bike route than you can use, so you have a many great options!

223

Just south of Tugman State Park is the little town of Lakeside, which connects the highway to the Tenmile Lake array of waterways. Not much of the town is visible on 101 as we ride through it, but a huge wooden signboard map depicting the Oregon Coast is midway through on the right, and shows you precisely where you are on this terrific bike ride. From here, it is only 12 easy and uneventful miles to the Coos Bay bridge.

The Coos Bay bridge is longer than the Yaquina Bay bridge.

This is the bridge that has struck fear deep into the hearts of many **Oregon Coast Bike Route** pilgrims over the years, and to read of these tales of dread, just visit **crazyguyonabike.com** and search for the Coos Bay bridge entries. Folks have said that to cross this bridge on a bike is as close to suicidal as one can imagine, so, living nearby, I decided to investigate their fears. To make a long story short, their many extreme worries were totally unfounded. That is to say, when you get here, just relax!

They said it was illegal to ride the car lane (it isn't). They said there wasn't enough room on the sidewalk to pedal or push a bike safely (there is). They said it can get windy up there (it can, so be prepared). You can use the sidewalk without **any** problem!

North Bend (MP 235) is a town of more than 10,000 residents, and it abuts the sister town of Coos Bay, which lies to its southern edge. Coos Bay is the largest city on the Oregon Coast, with over 16,000 sea loving souls living there. Combined with North Bend from a population standpoint, crossing the Coos Bay bridge puts a cyclist in a region with roughly 26,000 people, not a mega metro area, but large for the Oregon Coast at least.

North Bend is located in Coos County, and became a formal town in 1903. Prior to European immigrants claiming the Oregon Coast as their own, this area was inhabited by the Lower Umpqua, Coquille, Coos, and Siuslaw tribes, people who fished, hunted, and gathered for their existence. Francis Drake stopped here for a bit as he fled an ocean storm, and then headed north for all the other Oregon inlets we have toured. Around 1853, travel routes from inland were being created so people could reach this coastal area. As with other coastal towns, so isolated from anywhere, the easiest way to get here from places such as San Francisco was by sailing the Pacific Ocean. And, just like all the rest of them, once the Roosevelt Highway was built (AKA 101), folks were eager to experience this newly formed settlement.

COOS BAY BRIDGE ALTERNATE ROUTE

If you really don't want to cross this bay on this bridge, or, if you prefer to book on down to Bandon the absolute fastest and by far the easiest way possible, there is a simple and easy work-around alternate route that completely eliminates the busy towns of North Bend and Coos Bay, as well as eliminating the super steep Seven Devils route as advocated by the Adventure Cycling Association and the state of Oregon. In other words, you have choices here! It's entirely up to you! No pressure!

I offer this in response to the number of cyclists who have been very frightened of crossing the Coos Bay bridge, yet I really recommend taking the typical route as advocated by Adventure Cycling Association and the state of Oregon instead. This Coos Bay bridge has a sidewalk 40 inches wide, and I have ridden my fully loaded touring trike over it. This measurement was taken by me a while back, and I even photographed the tape measure for any doubters. It's over before you know it.

This sidewalk is the same width as the Yaquina Bay bridge, which we already crossed over up in Newport, but this bridge is longer.

If the wind is up, which is typical on the coast, simply get off your bike and walk it across. I recommend this route because of the sights you'll see along the way: the Cape Arago lighthouse, Sunset Bay and Shore Acres State Parks, and Seven Devils.

But, I do realize that we all have individual needs, or perhaps time schedules that translate into a quicker and more direct route, thus I shall briefly discuss what I call the Coos Bay bypass route, which is a rural road that goes around the east side of the bay, and rejoins OCH 101 south of the town of Coos Bay.

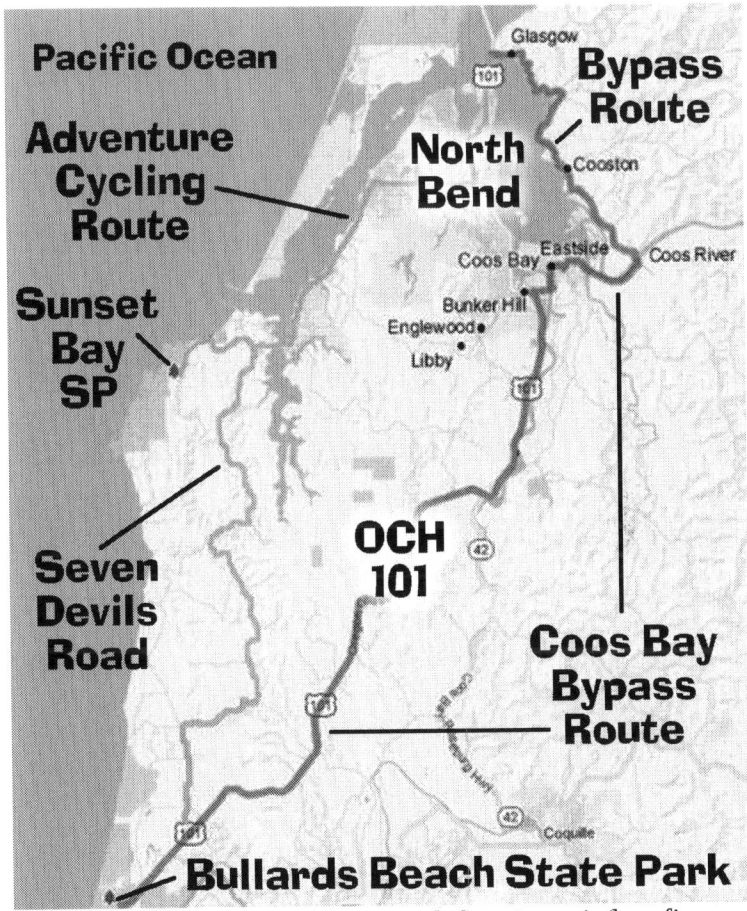

Both choices are similar mileages and elevation gain/loss figures.

Heading south on OCH 101, you will clearly observe the huge Coos Bay bridge long before you arrive at its northern entrance. After crossing some watery areas on the highway, the road heads uphill, and comes to a signal light. This light is your last chance to bail out of riding the bridge, which is immediately past the signal. At the signal, you will see a highway sign with these words written on it: EAST BAY DRIVE GLASGOW, and an arrow pointing to the left. So, as you approach the bridge and signal, move into the left hand turn lane to turn left on East Bay.

There is a small grocery store in Glasgow, less than a mile.

This is an easy and very relaxing rural alternative to the traffic encountered riding through North Bend on the way to the little fishing village of Charleston. East Bay Drive goes around the east side of the bay, as seen on the preceding map, through Glasgow and Cooston, both tiny little areas of human habitation, before it crosses a little bridge on the Coos River, and returns to 101 through the town of Eastside. Once you arrive back at OCH 101, just head south as we have been doing, and pedal on down to Bullards Beach State Park (MP 259) for camping. This is easy.

Rather than outlining this entire bypass route, which is not the way most cyclists travel, nor the formal **Oregon Coast Bike Route**, I will just direct you to a detailed article I wrote and posted on the Crazy Guy on a Bike website, where you will be greeted by numerous photos and detailed explanations of how to do it (quite simple actually). So, if this bypass sounds like something you would prefer, all you need do is visit this link: **http://www.crazyguyonabike.com/doc/12467**. This little bypass rejoins the normal bike route north of Bullards Beach State Park.

NORTH BEND TO CRANBERRY LAND

We shall stick to the **Oregon Coast Bike Route** and transport ourselves across the Coos Bay bridge. I choose not to call it by its current and formal name because of the man's shortsightedness in his design of it, along with all his other coastal bridges, casting the safety concerns of human powered folks to the wind. People on the Oregon Coast tend to dote over Conde McCullough's bridge designs, praising the aesthetics of them all, but of course, those same people drive cars over these bridges, with no idea of the stress felt by thousands of bicyclists each year.

After crossing the bridge on the sidewalk, at a leisurely pace to allow for the enjoyment of the elevated views (and some photos) we get to a little park setting just past a large railroad locomotive exhibit. This is called **Simpson Park**, and it is home to the Coos Historical Maritime Museum and the North Bend Visitor Center. There are restrooms here, and the setting is perfect for a little bit of relaxation and snacking.

Now, essentially what we are aiming to do is get from here out to the **Cape Arago Highway**, which will take us south and west towards the fishing village of **Charleston**, Sunset Bay State Park and Shore Acres State Park, Cape Arago lighthouse, and Cape Arago itself. Cape Arago is a dead-end, and requires doubling back to the **Seven Devils** road to be on track for Bandon, but this little diversion is so scenic and awesome that practically every cyclist to ever pedal this coastline opts to take it.

We have a couple of choices here. We can remain on OCH 101 for a few blocks and turn right on Virginia Avenue, following the signs to OCEAN BEACHES and Charleston. This is direct, and how the cars do it, but there is also traffic you may not wish to hassle. The other way is what most cyclists do, and that is to take the quiet residential streets at the south end of the park, south and west, zig-zagging, until we end up on Virginia Avenue, kind of past the worst of the traffic. Heading south and west out of the park may seem like a maze and challenge, and some books will describe turn-by-turn street names, but this is not really necessary for two reasons: First, you can only go a few blocks west before the roads turn south because of waterways, and second, you will run back into Virginia Avenue in a few blocks whether you know where you're going or not. Plus, it's signed as the **Oregon Coast Bike Route**. You won't get lost.

Then, you just head west on Virginia, past the Safeway market, until you reach the intersection of **Broadway**, where you hang a left and ride south for a mile or so until you reach **Newmark**, where you turn right (west). Some maps refer to Broadway and Newmark at part of the Cape Arago Highway, but in any event, once Newmark curves south at the Coos River, in a couple miles, you're set for Charleston on the **Cape Arago Hwy**.

Cape Arago Highway runs alongside the Coos River to the sea.

There is a draw bridge at Charleston. In twenty years I have never seen it in the up position, but on my 2013 coastal ride to southern California, it was UP. This is the view from my trike seat. Neat!

The Charleston town limit sign is on the draw bridge, nothing fancy like some of the northern coast towns we have ridden.

The ride out Cape Arago Highway is easy, and once the road curves around to the right at Charleston, you know you've arrived in the quaint fishing village by seeing the colossal **mound of oyster shells** over on the left side of the road (I guess they are oyster). This mound is here for all of eternity for some reason, but it's a landmark for cyclists who may be wondering if they had taken the wrong turn somewhere a few miles back. You will also know you are in Charleston from the sign at the draw bridge, and all the fishing boats off in the bay to the right. You'll like this!

Charleston is a little town, and even on a bike or trike, you're out the other side in a flash, where the road becomes an incline as you ride to Sunset Bay State Park for the night. Although, you can also put up your tent at **Bastendorff County Park**, a mile sooner, if you prefer a cliff overlooking the ocean, river, and jetty. Both campgrounds are great choices, however most cyclists opt to **camp at Sunset Bay** because it is on the Adventure Cycling Association list of places to stay. It is indeed very picturesque, with a cool little bay, and the main difference between it and Bastendorff is that the state park is tucked back in a dense forest with no views of anything except trees. Bastendorff provides a cliff overlook just a short walk from the tent.

Above, I am pitching my tent (standing on right), as the Oregon Coast Cycling Ghost (Matt Jensen) lays out his ground cloth. We both use small and very lightweight single-person tents for ease of travel. This is on the cliff at Bastendorff County Park, about a mile distant from Sunset Bay State Park. Both are good choices. Bastendorff has a steep hill to climb to access it though.

While you are here on Cape Arago, you may opt to also visit **Shore Acres State Park** and the end of Cape Arago where it places you prominently over the ocean with panoramic vistas of the ocean and surf. Shore Acres State Park is a day-use only park, but very much worth you visiting. Here, on particularly active surf days, the waves crash against jagged cliff faces, spewing whitewater sometimes up to ten stories tall! There are also beautiful **gardens** to amble through, and a short hike to Simpson beach! This incredible state park sits adjacent to Sunset Bay State Park, so it's all here in a neat and handy package for cyclists to see. Trust me – this is like a fairy tale ocean/land interface dream vision, truly worth your time! See it all, and take home memories!

Cape Arago is a short ride south past the Shore Acres entrance and is also a breathtaking place to experience! There are many **sea lions at Cape Arago**, audible for miles on the wind.

Shore Acres State Park is day-use, and REALLY worth it!

The Cape Arago lighthouse (above) is not accessible by normal civilian human beings, as it sits on a point and is guarded by a US Coast Guard fence. To see it as close as you can, find an overlook around the Sunset Bay State Park area, and get out your binoculars or camera's telephoto. This is the third lighthouse built here on Cape Arago, and the first two have been removed. The tower is 44 feet tall. In 1934 it was first lit. Of all the Oregon lighthouses, other than those two private ones, Cape Arago lighthouse is the most challenging to find. Good luck!

This is an aerial image of Simpson Beach, part of Shore Acres.

In 1948, Coos County gave the land that is now Sunset Bay State Park to the state of Oregon. Additional land was acquired through 1984. Water rights were obtained from a private person in 1954. Acres total just over 405, and total yearly camping visitation exceeds 68,000. As with many coastal state parks, the camping here is most definitely in the tsunami zone. If you feel an earthquake, go quickly to high ground! If you camp at Bastendorff County Park, you are tsunami safe already.

The original tract of land for Shore Acres State Park came from Louis and Lela Simpson in 1942. This included their house overlooking the ocean on a cliff, the tennis courts of which you can still walk upon if you visit here. Just imagine your own house with such a great view and all the peacefulness here. The

Simpson family called their home Shore Acres, and the state adopted their nomenclature. Sea Captain Asa Simpson was the founder of North Bend, when he sailed here in 1855. Asa and his sons were barons in the lumber and shipping industries, and owned the land between North Bend and Cape Arago. The park is 745 acres, and receives well over 200,000 visitors each year.

Here is a view of Simpson Beach from the hiking trail down to it.

Yes, a cyclist can bypass all this Cape Arago scenery, ambiance, and history, but that cyclist would be missing out on quite a lot! This diversion off 101 is **one of the best** on the coast!

The Cape Arago Highway dead-ends at the impressive Cape Arago **scenic viewpoint**, where there is a huge grassy open space and parking for cars. Trails can be walked down the cliffs to the beach that surrounds the cape. Sea lions frequent the north side of this viewpoint, and are quite loud due to their high numbers. The **sea lions** can be heard from Bastendorff County Park, Sunset Bay State Park, and everywhere else around this neck of the woods. You can get photos of hundreds of these sea creatures, and it is possible to get fairly close, so be careful. The offshore rocks at the cape are part of the Oregon Islands National Wildlife Refuge, and thus protected from human encroachment.

Okay, for **some idea on mileages**, let's begin at the intersection of Virginia Avenue with Broadway Street back in North Bend. That is where many refer to as the start of the Cape Arago Highway. So, from that intersection, it is a little over 8 miles to the village of Charleston. It is just over 10 miles to Bastendorff County Park, and almost 12 miles to Sunset Bay State Park. At nearly 13 miles is Shore Acres State Park, and the Cape Arago scenic overlook comes in at around 14 miles. So, when you reach the Virginia/Broadway signal intersection, you are only about 14 miles away from Cape Arago. You must only backtrack to Seven Devils road, this side of Charleston – easy!

Above is Cape Arago Highway as we pedal back towards the very quaint fishing village of Charleston. Bastendorff County Park is on the hill to the left of these two cyclists. Just prior to re-entering Charleston, we will be turning right onto the infamous **Seven Devils road**, which we will be pedaling south towards Bullards Beach State Park and Bandon. Until we re-emerge onto OCH 101, the roads remain lightly traveled like this. The Seven Devils road is steep and curvy, but also very peaceful and remote, making for really relaxed pedaling for several hours.

Turn south onto Seven Devils road at the Old Charleston School.

This is the beginning of the first devil, with six more to come!

The Seven Devils road is well known amongst coastal Oregon pedal pushers, and there are many opinions of it. If you are one of those who loves to pedal up steep inclines, this is your lucky day. If you are one of those who loves racing down steep declines, this is also your lucky day because you'll find them all between here and where we arrive back out at Highway 101, just north of Bullards Beach State Park.

As you will recall from the map earlier, this road takes us south just like 101 does, however, it winds up and down over steep little mountains, requiring lots of shifting of gears along the way, whereas 101 is more gradual for high speed automobiles. Even a car on Seven Devils can't go real fast due to the many tight curves, especially near this road's inception at Charleston. Large portions of this route have been clear-cut logged.

The South Slough National Estuarine Research Reserve will be passed towards the beginning of this most wonderful cycling experience. It is a 4,800 acre natural area located in the Coos estuary. The purpose of this research reserve is to improve the understanding and stewardship of Pacific Northwest estuaries and coastal watersheds. This is where salt and fresh waters mix. Behind the sign in the photo is an impressive and well equipped interpretive center for visitors, from which many hiking paths take explorers through varied habitats of the reserve. Peaceful!

In a way, the **clear-cut logging operations** here have opened up the vistas so that we can see how expansive these coastal mountains are. When pedaling in deep forest all the time, one does not get an inclusive impression of the landscape, but here in these open areas, that changes dramatically. Clear-cutting is a fact of life in Oregon mountains, and due to the heavy rainfall in the northwest, particularly the Pacific Northwest, the trees and forests grow back amazingly quickly. Many folks refer to the entire state of Oregon as the Pacific Northwest, but technically, this term is only used for the portion of the state that lies west of the spine of the Coast Range. East of the spine is the northwest.

Bicyclists always have a sense of humor and here, a considerate biker has spray pained "DEVIL #2 onto the pavement. Below is a typical view that we see from the road once up out of the valley.

Still on the way up, it's time to refuel our weary organic engines.

Turn right at Whiskey Run road to begin heading back down.

Okay, some general thoughts here: Seven Devils road is signed, and easy to navigate, but at one point along the way, the pavement does a sharp left curve, and is now referred to as West Beaver Hill road. We follow the pavement, because what happens here is that Seven Devils continues straight, but is dirt and gravel for many miles. Yes, it will exit at the same place we are going, but few cyclists wish to ride off the easy paved route! We will come back into Seven Devils road farther south.

So now we are heading southeast on West Beaver Hill road, and we remain on this road until we reach the intersection of **Whiskey Run road**, as seen in the photo. By the way, West Beaver Hill road is also known as Chrome Mountain road on some maps. There are not many intersections or choices up here, so what may seem a little confusing in this book becomes crystal clear on the road. When you arrive at the intersection signed Whiskey Run road, **turn right** and head on down the steep and tightly curved mountain to reunite with Seven Devils on the flat ground. All the devils are gone now. You can remain on West Beaver Hill road, but it will dump you out on OCH 101 much sooner than turning right on Whiskey Run road. **Turn right!**

At the flat intersection with Seven Devils road, hang a left or you will ride another mile to the ocean (can if you want a diversion). In short order, Seven Devils deposits us back onto 101, not far north of Bullards Beach State Park, which is just north of Bandon. We can camp at Bullards, see the Coquille lighthouse, and resupply food in Bandon. Easy pedaling to 101:

Bullards Beach State Park offers wide expanses of sandy beach, along with the Coquille River lighthouse, all a very short bike ride from your tent campsite if you stay at this state park. This is just north of Bandon, and a great option for the night.

Above is the Coquille River lighthouse, which is easily accessible by bike from Bullards Beach State Park on a flat paved jetty road along the beach. I took this photo from across the Coquille River in Bandon's Old Town district, on the south jetty. The lighthouse sits on the north jetty. This lighthouse, unlike the Cape Arago lighthouse, is open to the public to visit.

After rejoining Highway 101 from the Seven Devils road, we travel wide and easy shoulders south to MP 259, where Bullards Beach State Park is located. The short paved road into the state park is also where the Coquille River lighthouse is accessed. It is all signed well, so you won't miss any of it if you are interested. About a half mile south of the state park, we cross the Coquille River on a short flat bridge with no shoulder, just prior to entering the town of Bandon.

The Coquille River lighthouse began its life in 1891, and after numerous delays, was finally shining its light out to sea by 1896. In 1939, this lighthouse was abandoned due to new technology that automated a beacon for ships, but in 1976, it was fixed up by the Oregon State Parks and the US Army. In the late 1800s and early 1900s, ships kept slamming into the jetty despite the light. Well, as if by some bizarre sense of need, the natural world stepped in and really lit up the Coquille River and jetty when it set the Bandon town on fire, destroying nearly every building in it. This was a forest fire in 1936. This lighthouse was fired back up again in 1991, and is open to the public to visit.

Bullards Beach State Park exists on land acquired from private owners and the Bureau of Land Management (BLM). Robert Bullard, an early settler with his family, operated a store, post office, and made a way for folks to get across the river on his ferry business, which was where the present bridge on OCH 101 crosses the river at its narrowest point. The acreage of this state park is 1,289, and the annual overnight campers are about 94,000 people, some on bicycles and tricycles.

A word is in order here about about the milepost markers. **This is really weird**, but important for MP aficionados! They make an abrupt and **unexpected change** for those of us crazy enough to be watching them all. Most motorists pay absolutely no attention as they speed by so fast they don't even know they are there. Well, for lowly us on bikes and trikes, yes, we will notice that there is a mysterious **12 mile absence** of numbers that just disappear for no apparent reason. **Are we going crazy?**

Well, the reason is because 101 used to run inland to the small town of Coquille on a narrow and curvy path, and those extra 12 miles still haunt us. State routes 42 and 42S have taken over the old portions of US 101 around Coquille following the bypass. This reconstruction of 101 years ago shortened distances and eliminated those narrow curvy sections so it could run closer to the ocean, also allowing automobiles to go faster, which was essential to **boost Oregon's economy**. The road still goes to California regardless of what out of date MP signs may indicate.

Bandon is known as the **CRANBERRY CAPITAL** of Planet Earth – well, that's my take on it anyway, as some folks believe it's just the cranberry capital of Oregon. Little do they know how famous their town really is in the universe. Ocean Spray gets cranberries here, so yes, it's indeed big!

This is why this section of the books was headed **North Bend to Cranberry Land** – now you know my crazy reasoning. I eat pounds of these Bandon Cranberries every winter, stocking up from local farmers. Oh, and did you know that these berries are loaded with antioxidants to **make you immortal**? Yes, I eat them totally **raw** in cereals, yogurts, and things that need some enlivening. **They are tart, but you develop a taste!**

Anyway, back to Bandon! These cranberries are the community's #1 agricultural crop, and one reason why the 6,000 people of the greater area love to live here – they are all **crazy cranberry lovers**, people who go around with red tongues. The second week in September each year they celebrate with the annual Cranberry Festival, so plan your cycling tour for that time to cash in and get your share. The annual **Cranberry Queen** is crowned during these festivities. Well, you get the picture. This place is loaded with cranberry bogs and **red tongues**. Oh, and it has a really awesome Old Town district you just gotta' see!

Now, despite what anyone else may tell you, or what you may read on some map or in some book, **don't turn right** off OCH 101 at the intersection of Riverside Drive just prior to MP 260. Some guidebooks may say this will get you down near the river on a little rural road, which indeed it will, and will take you into Old Town, which indeed it will, but it will also cause you to miss Ray's Food Place, a large market with nice restrooms, plenty of groceries, and a sit-down deli. What cyclist in their right mind would pass up a perfectly good food source? Not you!

So, when you hit **Riverside Drive**, just keep on bookin' south on 101, on the super huge shoulders and flat road, and turn in at Ray's Food Place at the north of town to replenish whatever you need. Unless it has changed, the celebrated ACA bike route **bypasses both** Bandon markets, which includes Price 'n Pride on the south end of town. Also, if you're a health food nut like I am, you'll also miss Mother's Natural Foods and Grocery around the curve south of Ray's! Oh my gosh, what were the route planners thinking? The "Everything Cookie" at Mother's is absolutely the most nutritious and filling cookie you'll ever eat!

What you do is this: Pass Riverside Drive, pedal a little farther into the town proper, stop at Ray's and Mother's, and THEN drop down the hill just past Mother's and turn right into Old Town. All you missed by doing this little alternate thinking is passing the **sewage plant on Riverside Drive** – probably not something you wanted to see anyway! You've missed nothing.

And don't forget, Bandon shows at MP 274, for whatever it's worth. Of course, I suppose ODOT (Oregon Department of Transportation) will finally go out and change all the milepost markers around after I write this, thereby invalidating these notes of mileages on the southern coast, but hey, that's how the cranberry pops! No big deal. Just keep on pedaling south.

Ray's Food Place during a very rare coastal rain. It will be dry when you get here, so dismiss any notion of rain gear and cold.

Mother's Natural Grocery is about a 2 minute pedal from Ray's, just around the bend at the first light in Bandon. I always stop here right after Ray's because Mother's deli is healthy and delicious. What I do is buy general groceries at Ray's Food Place, and then eat my health lunch at Mother's Natural Grocery. Just past this little health store, OCH 101 goes down a hill, and at the bottom, you'll see Old Town on your right. Turn right and enjoy!

My recommendation is to follow the Adventure Cycling route from Old Town forward, as it takes cyclists along the world famous **high cliffs of Bandon**, where you can see and explore incredible sea stacks, big rocks that stick straight up out of the wet sandy beach! Check out the following photos:

Hiking amongst the bizarre rock formations at Bandon is fun!

This feels like "Journey to the Center of the Earth".

How would this driftwood look in your front yard?

People are dwarfed when climbing through the rock crevices.

This is called **Beach Loop road**, and everyone who ever visits this area travels it to see such an impressive concentration of many sea stacks in one easy location. You can walk down long stairways and walk amongst these giants, exploring hidden caves, or you can remain on top and just take a bunch of photographs like most fat and unfit car tourists do. Cycling is enough exercise!

So, after you get food at Ray's and Mother's, and are pedaling around Old Town, having missed the sewer treatment facility, take 1st Street around the curve to 4th Street, which kind of becomes 7th Street. This is also known as Ocean Drive, and it comes to a cliff, thereby doing a left curve to morph into Beach Loop road. You pedal past Face Rock, also mindfully aware of all the bizarre sea stacks to your right, and then about two miles farther south the loop curves back to Highway 101. Wonderful!

WHERE IS SOUTH BEND?

Okay now, we've been through North Bend, which, by its name would tend to indicate that there may be a sister city of South Bend, but where the devil is it? Hmm, I must have devils on the mind, having just pedaled over seven of them. Anyway, what gives with this north/south naming stuff? Here is the answer you've been waiting for: There is no South Bend. It just happens that the town we now call North Bend was created on the north bend of the Coos River, thus its naming. Simple! Now you know.

BANDON TO CAPE BLANCO

Once back on 101, keep an eye out for the cranberry bogs that are visible from the highway shortly before MP 283. Cranberries were so named because some European settlers in what is now commonly called America thought the complete plant looked like the neck, head, and bill of a crane bird. Did you know that? Since I eat many pounds of these raw berries every year, for their antioxidant qualities, I figured I just had to know where the weird name originated. Yes, cranberries will extend our life spans as cyclists, as will blueberries, dried plums, and many other superfoods that wipe out free radicals. So, I love Cranberry Land.

Anyway, cranberries grow in dry beds, and then when it nears time to harvest, these beds become wet bogs because the farmers flood them with water. This flooding makes it easier to harvest these little red jewels that contribute so much to health nuts like me, and probably you too. See if you can spot the bogs, or beds if you pedal through too early in the season, when you are in this neck of the woods.

Once we have left the Bandon area, the road is inland enough that the ocean becomes a distant image of our minds for quite a ways, yet the miles zoom by quickly if you wish them to because the riding is easy this far south. We don't hit another monster cape until we leave Gold Beach, south of MP 330, which seems like a world away, and even more so if you camp at Cape Blanco State Park or Humbug Mountain State Park tonight (meaning you hit the cape tomorrow sometime).

The shoulders are fine, and cycling this stretch is really pretty **laid back and peaceful**, with wood carving shops right on the highway to distract you as the hours roll by. Not far past MP 285, we cross the Coos County line as we enter Curry County, a county that has been down on its financial luck in recent times. Yep, I guess governments can indeed go bankrupt – gee just look at the US government to know this.

The accepted pronunciation is Lang-less, not Lang-loy. Just sayin'

The little village of Langlois arrives around MP 288, give or take a few tenths, and since I don't give a whipper snapper's eyelash for tenths of a mile, I shant be getting any more precise than that. We are out here riding a long highway of pavement through beautiful country, and fixating on mileages is the **last** thing we want to be doing. The only reason I mention this stuff is because this is a guide book, and readers tend to expect some guidance now and then (especially those folks who use high tech satellite GPS imaging on a ride as simple as this).

Above is the market that offers **free water** bottle fill-ups for cyclists in Langlois. The town is tiny, and this market is one of the few businesses still in business here. Most have given up these days, so give 'em your money for something! And while you're in there, fill up your water bottles in the back room. This place is surprisingly busy for such a wide spot in the highway.

About a mile south of Langlois, you have a camping option if you wish to escape OCH 101 for a while. It's a loop road, and adds perhaps 5 miles to the trip, but Floras Lake, and the Boice-Cope campground, part of the Curry County parks, is a small and relaxing setting literally on the edge of a little lake next to the surf of the big blue ocean. I used to come here to windsurf. Windsurfers like this little lake because you can literally walk to the ocean side if you are tall, because the lake is very shallow all the way across. The cost is $14 for a tent site, which if shared with other cyclists, is great. There is also free Wi-Fi in this quiet campground next to the lake and ocean. It's a secret locale! Don't tell! Stay here one night, and then it's an easy ride to Cape Blanco State Park for the next night – you'll arrive early enough to do some hiking over to the cliffs and lighthouse – cool!

Boice-Cope campground, of Curry County Parks, is a very quiet hidden getaway on Floras Lake. It is first come, first served.

Past Langlois and the Floras Lake loop, the highway continues large and wide and easy, with its grand shoulders and gorgeous scenic vistas of forests and farmlands. If you're in a hurry, you'll enjoy this, but if not, settle in for a nice afternoon. If you camp at Boice-Cope, you're home already for tonight, if not, you are either going to get a motel in Port Orford, camp at the popular Humbug Mountain State Park, **OR** ... if you follow this book's **required official route**, you're almost ready to bed down because you should camp tonight at Cape Blanco State Park.

The next town you shall see a sign for is Denmark (MP who knows), which got its name because many of the earliest immigrant settlers from the east and Europe came from the country of Denmark. There isn't much here, at least as viewed from the highway. This is farm and ranch country, and beyond your view on 101 are many working ranches, some of which you can see while pedaling along, up on the hillsides. The next town, a few miles south of Denmark, is called Sixes. It has a grange visible as you pedal south, but also seems just a wide spot in the road. Now where did that name originate? Okay, here's the secret scoop, only found in this crazy and weird cycling guide:

The first inhabitants of this land called it Sik-ses-tine, which in our tongue means 'people by the far north country'. When the **gold** mine frenzy began here (yes, there's lots of it on the Sixes River), the miners shortened this to Sikhs, which meant 'friend' in the Chinook language. I suppose that would sound like 'sixes' when pronounced, so the oral way of saying it eventually translated to an easy English version we now call Sixes.

A guy pedaling a tricycle near Cape Blanco Highway

See how wide and easy the riding is out here south of Bandon? The southern coast, south of Coos Bay, has no highways coming in from the interior of the state, as do the towns of the northern coast, thus inland Oregonians visit less. The major metro areas of Portland, Salem, and Eugene keep the north shores very busy and touristy. Down here, the large Coast Range has no roads to let the swarms of humanity overrun the place, **thus this quiet.**

255

This gorgeous horse saw me pedaling my trike, and looked over.

You might recall how we began this Oregon Coast cycling trip, up and out on the northwestern most point in the state, a secret spot that nearly every normal biker or triker misses all together! Well, I happen to enjoy these little out-of-the-way secret places, so I seek them out, and then choose to share them quietly to a few select pedal pushers such as yourself in these pages. That is the reason I spent time divulging the knowledge and location of Floras Lake – you might like it too!

Well, fellow cyclists, get ready for **our next secret**, only this is a BIG one that you are **required to visit**, simply because you have chosen to acquire this weird little book and read it. If word gets back that you have opted to miss this next **golden gem** of the Oregon Coast, then you are grounded from your bike or trike for the next 365 days, **and your trip didn't count**.

So, we just pedaled out of Sixes, what there was of it anyway, and now are beginning to go up a little incline after crossing the bridge that spans the Sixes River. By the way, there is still plenty of gold dust to be pulled from this river upstream a few miles, near the Edson area very primitive camping sites. You probably don't want to pedal up there – too far, not really worthy.

257

Getting on, 48 meters higher in elevation than the Sixes River bridge (the bridge is an elevation of 7 meters above the ocean level, and the turnoff is an elevation of 55 meters) is our next turn, and a great campground and incredible place await us!

Look for the sign that reads **Cape Blanco State Park**, and **hang a right** at the intersection when you arrive, which is at the top of the 55 meter hill. But, you say, "I am on a time schedule for this bike trip, and I must remain on 101." Well, to that I retort "You're reading this book ahead of time so you can makes plans in advance that allow for this deviation from due south." In other words, there is **no** truly acceptable **excuse** here, because this is a **rare opportunity** to say you've been to a rare geographical place on Planet Earth!

Or at least on the Oregon Coast! Yes, my friends, Cape Blanco is indeed the **farthest west** a land-bound human being can travel in this state, and besides that, out here Oregon's 1870 lighthouse still stands as an active beacon for seafaring fishing folks. It is roughly six miles out to the end of the huge cliff of the cape, where the quiet campground awaits us, and the views are spectacular. You can remember this distance because we just passed Sixes, the magic number. This turnoff is four miles north of Port Orford, the next town of normal coastal size.

What cyclist in his or her right mind would come out and ride the Oregon Coast, but then miss the farthest west portion of it because of not wishing to ride the extra 12 miles? Hey, ya' just don't do that! **NO** it's not an option for us! Besides all this heavy-handed persuasion going on, the Cape Blanco lighthouse is the

final official state lighthouse on the Oregon Coast (there is one in Brookings, but it's private, and so does not count). This diversion is one of those "**must do**" affairs, just as the Three Capes Scenic Loop is, and also the Otter Crest Loop. Nuf sed.

If all those reasons aren't enough, history buffs will most definitely need to visit and tour the world famous Hughes House, which sits on the final hill before the road levels at the cape. It overlooks the ocean out back. This Victorian home was built in 1898, and saved from destruction years ago by the historical societies who pledged to renovate it for visitors. When you see this place, you'll think how very incredibly fortunate the Hughes family was to live and work here, a primitive locale back then. There are many hiking trails between here and the campground.

Blanco means white in Spanish, and thus the Spanish Explorer Martin D'Aguilar, who was sailing his ship around here in 1603, decided to name this cape "blanco" when he beheld the whitish chalky appearance of the headlands from the ocean. A few years after Martin D'Aguilar was here, about 295 to be approximately precise, the Irish Hughes clan acquired a couple thousand acres here to live and run a seaside dairy operation, among other things. Well, Oregon purchased this land from the Hughes estate in 1971, and now YOU can come here as a lowly bicyclist and be where Spanish explorers and wealthy land barons once hung out! Once here, you will definitely understand why.

This headland rises to 245 feet above the salt water below, and the light from the Cape Blanco lighthouse is visible from 22 miles out on the ocean. Records reveal many ship wrecks occurring on this cape in past times. Gee, this Oregon coastline has sure been the ruin of many a fine sailing vessel. How many ships are now using it as a **graveyard**? How many **ghost ships** are buried in the sands beneath our feet? Plenty!

A word about Ireland, or at least about an Irishman who came from there in the 1800s: Patrick Hughes first became enamored with this scenic cape in 1860, and his expansive spread kept the land fairly wild until Oregon acquired it for this state park. Cape Blanco State Park is just over 1,895 acres in size, and about 35,000 people camp here every year, a number to which you will add your mark while on this trip! **You must opt in.**

This distant view of the Cape Blanco lighthouse is from the north, looking across a small bay from one of many hiking trails. There are hot showers in the campground, and lots of bunnies.

Cape Blanco lighthouse awaits you, along with a gift shop.

North of the lighthouse is this trail that heads down and curves around to the historic Hughes house. This place can get windy.

Big spires like this massive monolith await you and your camera. You've come a long way on this coastal Oregon journey, and to miss Cape Blanco is to miss a **big** key element of this ride!

Off shore a little farther away are these sea stacks, like a minefield waiting for unsuspecting ships, thus the need for the Oregon houses of light. I don't know about you, but the large rock on the right sure looks like a whale swimming along! You'll love this place, a **universe away** from what you know as reality.

The hiking trails provide immense and wondrous views all along.

Most of the Cape Blanco campsites are sheltered from potential wind by dense shrubbery, making it easier to pitch a tent. There is no noise out here except for the crashing ocean surf on the beach.

WILD WINDS ON THE OREGON COAST

Does it get very windy here? Well, yes, at times, some say most of the times, wind does play a prominent factor in this coastal landscape. After all, winds are the primary reason we ride from north to south, because big winds tend to push us along that way during the summer months, and this is important when ascending the many huge capes and heads. Damn straight it gets windy!

Do you recall earlier photographs in this book of the trees that are all deformed along the headlands? That is because during the winter, the winds shift from northwest to southwest, and that is when they truly **begin to howl**. It gets spooky enough that you don't want to be outside. Keep in mind that during the winter it also rains, and when extreme winds and heavy rains combine, it is indeed a show to behold! One of the main things to do here in the winter months is to watch the severe winter storms.

The reason I am putting this little section on wind at this late point in the book is because Cape Blanco has experienced the strongest winds recorded on the coast, but not really by a large factor, because once triple digits are hit and surpassed, it pretty much feels the same: It will blow the man down! There are many places on the **Oregon Coast Bike Route** that have winds passing 100 miles per hour, or 160 kilometers per hour – that's cranking!

Okay, so here are some wind numbers to ponder as you sit all cozy and dry in your reading chair. Or, if you happen to be camping right now at Cape Blanco State Park, and are hunkered down in your tent while reading these words during a raging wind storm, you'll truly understand what it's all about!

WIND SPEEDS ON RECORD:
(highest winds are usually on the headlands)

Cape Blanco:	179 MPH
Newport:	138 MPH
Florence:	119 MPH
Astoria:	096 MPH
North Bend:	081 MPH
Brookings:	063 MPH

These wind numbers are not representative of the normal experiences on the Oregon Coast. Stuff like this does not happen frequently – they are the extremes because folks love all the bad news – it's more exciting (unless you're caught in it). Since we are riding our bikes and trikes in the summer, our experiences are mundane by comparison. It would be a great story to tell if one of those 179 MPH gusts dropped in behind my trike while pedaling up Neahkahnie Mountain though! Guess I could just coast up.

CAPE BLANCO TO GOLD BEACH

Well girls and boys, as incredible and relaxing as Cape Blanco is, with all its majestic vistas and magic memories, the time has come to move along towards California, that late great state to the south of here. And hey, we really are not too far at this point, especially considering our excitement of capturing that one special photograph all Oregon Coast cyclists long to have in their image gallery: the iconic "Welcome to California" sign.

We will be passing through the rural Port Orford on our way to the more full featured Gold Beach, a stretch of about 38 miles from out here on the **farthest west point** in Oregon. We've been at the state's most northwestern point, and now at the state's most western point, so all we have to experience on this particular ocean ride is the coast's **most southern point**. All 3 we **must** do!

After we pedal the six miles back to OCH 101 (recall we are off on the Cape Blanco State Park entrance road currently), we hang a right, and head south again, past acres of agricultural farm and ranch land. The road is wide and easy. It is less than 4 miles to Port Orford this morning, where we can hit the grocery.

Having passed the Elk River, we arrive in Port Orford, a town that claims it's the oldest on the Oregon Coast, and the most westerly in the lower 48 states of the US. It was platted in 1851, so it has indeed been here for a while!

This picturesque rural setting remains a functional fishing port, and you will observe the fishing vessels if you ride up the steep hill at the south end of the main street, and overlook the ocean and marinas below. You will recognize this short residential hill because of the huge words painted on the pavement across the width of the road. They read: **OCEAN VIEW**, with an arrow pointing straight ahead. It's only about a two block diversion off 101, and is worth the look over the south coast to California.

Being this far south on Highway 101, Port Orford is not subject to the extremely high traffic levels as are the small towns on the north coast, such as Cannon Beach. This is a quieter feel, more peaceful. Port Orford Heads State Park sits on the headland with its lifeboat station museum. It's a great hiking trail.

There exists a very active artist's community here, with 8 galleries of local artists, and for the painters amongst them, the sunsets and waves provide plenty of subject matter. The folks here see themselves in transition between the past of the fishing and lumber industries, and the future, which is primarily now fishing. There is an endangered tree in these parts called the Port Orford cedar, and this is high on residents' minds.

Just as we are heading out of town after the road curves to the east, we pass Battle Rock Wayside Park, whee it is said that a battle occurred between the first people of this area and the new incoming settlers who wanted the land for their own. There is a visitor center here, and you will also notice black beach sand if the trail to the water is followed to the large sea stack. From this wayside on out to MP 306, there are several turnout vista points that make for some excellent ocean and sea stack photographs, along with pictures back northwest towards Port Orford.

Up ahead there is another outstanding place to camp if you want to spend time exploring Port Orford today (it would be too soon to camp, having just left Cape Blanco). Past MP 305 we enter Humbug Mountain State Park, where the road ascends up onto the side of some steep headlands, although the rise here is not so challenging as most of the headlands we've come across.

    A fog slowly creeps in from the Pacific, onto the highway and headlands of Humbug Mountain State Park. The sun of just a few moments ago silently fades, and we are enshrouded in mystic ambiance of whispering waves gently lapping the sandy beach.

The Civilian Conservation Corps began developing this state park in 1934, on lands acquired from Carl White in 1926. and other state purchases. Acquisition of land for Humbug went through 1975. The overnight camping section, which is worthy of a biker's stay, was developed in 1952. In 1958, a large forest fire burned much of the park's northern section. Total acreage is 1842 and total yearly campers exceed 30,000 people.

There is a prominent form of land here called Humbug Mountain, which was originally called Sugarloaf Mountain. Then in 1851, the bungles of a survey party looking for an eastward passage through the Coast Range to the state's interior, earned the unwelcomed moniker of Humbug, meaning impostor or fake, as there was no easy passage through the extensive mountains and dense forests. There is a 3 mile loop trail that hikers can explore to the top of Humbug Mountain, but despite its height above the ocean, no ocean views are to be found at the top due to thick and overgrown foliage and forest. Only partway up the trail can a tiny short peek northward be seen if a person is searching for views.

The camping facilities here are very nice, with modern and private showers, typical of the 16 coastal Oregon State Parks that provide for overnight camping. The hiker/biker campsites are up in the dirt on the side of a hill, probably an after-thought based on its distance to the bath facilities and its odd carved-out shape, but if two or more cyclists join forces, you can just get a regular campsite across from the main shower facility by the host, and it is then paved for the few yards to the shower! Can't beat that.

Sounds of 101 and the ocean can be heard (also Bigfoot at 2AM).

No, there are no Pacific Ocean views at the summit of this hike, just a small cleared area surrounded by dense brush and forest.

Only a brief coastal view is found partway up the hiking trail.

A standard campsite is the better option at Humbug Mountain SP.

The road up the tight canyon from the camping is very curvy, as it heads south to the Rogue River and popular resort Gold Beach.

Pampas grass grows wild along the Oregon and California coasts.

At MP 313, this sight will be waiting around a right hand curve! Who could resist pedaling over to get this photograph with the tyrannosaurus and brachiosaurus at Prehistoric Gardens Park?

Prehistoric Gardens is a family owned facility, with acres of life sized dinosaurs mixed in through the forest! You pay a fee, and then are free to roam the paths through the huge trees. The feeling is one of a prehistoric time, as you forget you are even on the highway. Placards describe these **ancient monsters**, and there is a gift shop. They combine nature, science, and adventure. This park is not just for children! Adults will learn a lot in the bargain.

Here is some history behind this unique Oregon business, as stated by the family: "Prehistoric Gardens is the vision of the late E.V. 'Ernie' Nelson, artist, sculptor, entrepreneur, and dinosaur enthusiast. In 1953 after working as a CPA and owning a mill machinery supply business, Nelson packed up the family and headed south from Eugene, Oregon to find a location to build his **Dinosaur Park**. He settled on a prehistoric rainforest on the Southern Oregon Coast and began the building process. After three years of construction, one trip to the Smithsonian in NYC and endless research to ensure the life-size replicas were scientifically correct, Nelson opened his **Prehistoric Gardens** on January 1st 1955. He would go on to construct 23 dinosaurs in total over the next 30 years.

"The Dinosaurs at Prehistoric Gardens are scientifically correct restorations, authentic in detail and restored in as life-like manner as possible. The Dinosaurs' size and shape are based on measurements of the mounted fossil skeletons displayed in the larger natural history museums of the United States. Exactly 23 Dinosaurs in total. Ranging from the flying Pteranadon with a wingspan of 27 feet, to the massive Brachiosaurus that towers 46 feet off the ground, the Prehistoric Gardens is chalk full of those awesome animals that disappeared from the face of this earth over **70 million years ago**! Alongside each Dinosaur exhibit is a plaque that contains fun facts about the dinosaur. Did you know the Stegosaurus had a brain the size of a peanut? The Dinosaur Tracks lead the way as you walk among these massive creatures. Self-guided tours allow you to see the dinosaurs at your own pace and even take a second trip around if you wish."

Learn more at **prehistoricgardens.com** and see the short introductory movie of what to expect here. Okay, to answer your question, no, I'm not on the payroll. Being a dinosaur fanatic as a kid, I just really get into stuff like this! Following is a brief talk of

Oregon's paleontology, the study of truly ancient life as measured by the human lifespan. This excerpt can be found on Wikipedia:

"No Precambrian fossils are known from Oregon, so the state's fossil record does not begin until the Paleozoic. No rocks are known in Oregon from the Cambrian to the Silurian, although the state was probably submerged by the sea. From the Devonian to the Permian a chain of volcanic islands began forming in the state. These islands were home to lagoons and surrounded by coral reefs. Brachiopods also inhabited the nearby waters. Plant fossils suggest a rich terrestrial flora was not far away. Oregon remained mostly covered in seawater throughout the Mesozoic. Local marine invertebrate life included corals, oysters, and snails. Local vertebrates included ichthyosaurs and pterosaurs. Although it has been claimed that no dinosaurs are known to have inhabited Oregon, fossils of a possible hadrosaurid ('duck-billed' dinosaur) were discovered in the southwestern corner of the state, believed to be Campanian in age. During the Cretaceous period, between 90 and 100 million years ago, most of Oregon was covered by the ocean. Plesiosaurs swam and fed on the fish of this Oregonian ocean.

"Oregon remained partially covered by the sea into the Cenozoic. Contemporary marine life included fig and turret-shelled snails. During the Tertiary, Oregon trees like Alniphyllum, ash, beech, cinnamon, Gargura, hemlock, hickory, hornbeam, oak, persimmon, pine, redwood, and sycamore grew in Oregon. Alders were also present. The most common local trees were the redwoods and sycamores. The Tertiary petrified wood of Oregon is sometimes partially opalized. Oregon's sea levels fluctuated rapidly during the Eocene to Oligocene interval. Mollusks were diverse in Oregon during the Eocene, with at least 25 species known from the Fern Ridge Dam area. From the Eocene to the Oligocene, the Sunset Highway area was covered in seawater. During this interval it was inhabited by invertebrates like crinoids, crustaceans, echinoderms, gastropods, and scaphopods. Local Eocene sharks left their teeth behind in the Rocky Point Quarry to the west of the Nehalem River. Crocodiles lived in Oregon from 60 to 45 million years ago"

Nope, no tyrannosaurus remains have been found here.

But you can see what they looked like at Prehistoric Gardens!

Now then, let's leave those dinosaurs where they were and get back to the present day! The highway remains wide and easy as we pass the little village area of Ophir at MP 317, which consists primarily of a sparsely inhabited residential setting at the beach. It is so minimal that you may not even realize you have been through it unless you look closely, for such signs indicating a golf course and Honey Bear campground. Euchre Creek enters the ocean at Ophir, yet another clue you are here.

Not far past MP 322 is the Geisel Monument Sate Park, a day-use facility that documents the final resting place for people who lost their lives at what is called the Rogue Indian War of 1856. The Geisel family gravesites are here at this state park. We are about seven miles north of Gold Beach, and after a few more laid-back miles, we approach the Old Coast road that is between the Otter Point State Recreation area and Gold Beach.

The state of Oregon officially recommends taking this side diversion off OCH 101, which will allow access to what is known as the Miner's Fort, which was occupied by local residents during the Indian wars where the Geisel family met their demise. This road loop is also known as the Wedderburn loop, and it rides along the Rogue River more closely than does 101 above, until the Rogue River bridge is reached, where it rejoins the highway for crossing into the town of Gold Beach.

We find ourselves in Gold Beach somewhere in the area of MP 328. You can see the town from the north side of the river where it hits the Pacific. Oregon's largest myrtlewood tree is to be found about 10 miles up the Rogue River. How do you get up there? As you will discover from local billboard advertising, the popular way is on **Jerry's Rogue Jets**, large supercharged boats that take visitors up the Rogue at high speeds with high thrills! They have 64, 80, and 104 mile **jet boat treks** for those bold few who opt to climb on board. More than 35,000 people do this each year, and see wildlife, including **black bears** in the shore water! The jet boats can travel in as little as 8 inches of water, which is useful to navigate the rapids on the longer rides upriver. Jerry's began in 1958, the first commercial jet boat tours in the United States. Learn the full story and see the movie at: **roguejets.com**.

In 1853, after the California gold discoveries of 1849, the mineral was also found where the Rogue River empties into the Pacific Ocean. Well, of course we know what disease lots of men get when this occurs – **GOLD FEVER!** True to form, gold was blurring the rational thought processes of many a man in those days, and they flocked to this precise spot in droves, established a town called Ellensburg, and it grew like the proverbial weed. The fighting with the first inhabitants of this region then ensued, but once they were obliterated from the record, the newly formed Curry County made Gold Beach the county seat.

Jerry's Rogue River Jet boats offer wild thrills and memories!

Crossing the Rogue River is flat, with high visibility, an easy ride over the bridge. If you seek an adrenaline spike, Jerry's Jet boats are right around the corner after this river crossing.

At the south end of the Rogue River bridge you will have no doubt where you are, as you see this large and colorful ornate sign for Gold Beach, a popular south coast vacation mecca.

This triker just crossed the bridge, and is on the hill into town. Jerry's Jet boats is back at the bottom of this hill, just past bridge.

As with all the frenetic operations set up by men seeking a quick way to financial riches, the **real money** was made by the far-sighted folks who moved in to support the delusions of crazy prospectors who just knew they were going to strike it rich. It was these support industries that led to lasting establishment of what is now called Gold Beach. Fishing, logging, merchandising of the supplies needed by miners grew the wilderness town quickly.

Gold mining dwindled rather quickly, as expected, with a decline in fur trapping and logging following over the years. Fish held a prominent place in the minds of entrepreneurs who stayed around subsequent to the evacuation of the miners and trappers, but by 1935, the commercial fishing had pretty much wiped out the indigenous fish, so the state stepped in and passed legislation to outlaw its continuance. Things were looking dim, except …

It was becoming clear that tourists seeking wilderness and beach getaways had indeed struck gold in Gold Beach. All those support industries that provided for the **greedy gold seekers** have long since morphed into welcoming tourists and retirees!

Hubby fixes his wife's broken spoke, a temporary bugaboo.

GOLD BEACH TO CALIFORNIA

Certain towns have a big surprise awaiting cyclists not far south of their city limits. That is why reading guidebooks like this can remove the element of surprise. Of course, sometimes it may be better not to know what lies ahead, so one's head doesn't get all messed up with worry. What I can say is this: Stop at the market in Gold Beach and eat quite a bit of **calorie-rich food** prior to continuing on this gorgeous bike route!

The big surprises, which get a cyclist's attention in a big way, come in the form of Steep Hilly Intense Terrain, and now after many miles of easy southern coastal pedaling, **the party is finally over**! Time to test your mettle and gearing once again!

These identical circumstances occurred after Cannon Beach several days back, as well as the towns of Tillamook, Neskowin, Yachats, and Charleston. There may be other places you might wish to include in this list. Prepare yourself for some steep and very long inclinage. Sebastian and Samuel are coming!

South of Gold Beach are a few sea stacks, which seem to always be very popular with sea birds! Five of them saw me pedal by.

Yep, there it is! There is no getting around it except to climb up.

Leaving Gold Beach, the riding is easy for a while, and, as nearly always, the vistas are spectacular, with lots of ocean out to our right, and always the sounds of crashing surf. The climbing begins in short order, and we lose views of the ocean as we pedal through forests, which, on a sunny day at certain times, helps to keep the heat off. There are false summits on this ascent, where you think the top is near, only to find more coming your way.

A high point is reached at **Bellview Lane**, which happens to be the perfect place to stop for an energy bar and lots of water, if you haven't been eating all the way up. This is an especially tough climb on warmer days, but it does peak here. I have called this Bellview Hill, and from here, we get a little reprieve for a bit.

In the vicinity of MP 334, we enter the Cape Sebastian Scenic Corridor, the first of two very incredible state parks just north of California. This park land is said to be named to honor a saintly fellow of the early 1600s, named, as you might guess, Sebastian. There are viewpoints where you can pull in for photos. These are on the descent from Bellview Lane, and you may enjoy stretching your legs at scenic vista points. The views are great.

This resting place on Cape Sebastian is 718 feet above sea level!

The Cape Sebastian Scenic Corridor land was obtained by Oregon between 1925 and 1963. In the 1930, the CCC began developing the area, as they did for many of the Oregon coastal parks during that time period. There is a popular story associated with this place, where, in 1942, a caretaker was making a routine check of some trails on a heavily fogged day, and he heard voices near the bottom of the cape's cliff. There was a very brief clearing of the fog for a moment, so the caretaker looked far below to see a **Japanese submarine** at the surface, which, according to his own accounting, was recharging its batteries.

Apparently, the Japanese Pacific Fleet was hanging out at American beaches during the second world war of the early 40s, as learned while gathering historical accounts for this book. The first we learned of this was up at Clatsop Spit, where the Japanese commander Tagami Meiji piloted his submarine into the mouth of the Columbia River, and is reported to have lobbed seventeen explosive shells at Fort Stevens before American war planes were able to fly out and drop some bombs on his location. Tagami was a crafty fellow however, and avoided destruction and capture.

Recumbent trikes hit 50 MPH on that descent – what a thrill!

Sea stacks await us south of Cape Sebastian, prior to Pistol River.

The Samuel H. Boardman State Scenic Corridor arrives not too far south of Pistol River, a former hangout for windsurf devotees. The land for this state scenic area was acquired between 1949 and 1957. The fellow for whom this corridor is named was the first Oregon State Parks superintendent, and he served in this position for a whopping 21 years, from 1929 to 1950. In the early 1940s, he proposed the creation of a scenic area in Curry County, but the idea was not popular enough to become established. Later, this current scenic corridor was created, and named after Sam.

The corridor is about 12 miles long, north to south, and is mostly high cliffs with spectacular rock formations and forests right next to OCH 101. I recommend taking the time to pull out at the signed viewpoints because you'll see some awesome sights that will get your camera pointing and clicking. You'll see places like Arch Rock, Natural Bridges, and House Rock – all incredibly scenic and forever memorable, showcasing once again on this 383 mile journey why nearly everyone votes the Oregon Coast as the most breathtaking of the entire Pacific ride in the western US.

It is easy, and sometimes tempting if you are tired already, to ride right on by the overlooks. <u>Resist</u> that temptation – **take** the time!

You will love the unique rock formations along this corridor!

A few areas are more open and rocky appearing. It's ALL great!

The northern border of the Samuel H. Boardman State Scenic Corridor is roughly 15 miles north of Brookings, the final town prior to California, and the southern border is only 3 miles north of Brookings. These are 12 miles to truly appreciate as we close in on our journey's destination. There is one location called Indian Sands in this corridor where archaeological study has been successful at determining human activity here **12,000 years ago**, of nomadic travelers who crossed the Bering land bridge between today's Russian area and America's Alaskan region.

MP 348 is nearby. You should park and look over the edge here!

The bridge is flat and easy, with high visibility, and no dangers.

The Thomas Creek bridge is within the boundaries of the Samuel Boardman State Scenic Corridor, and was opened for use in1961. I wonder how folks crossed prior to this bridge. The span is 105 meters above the creek below (345 feet), and the length from end to end is 113 meters (371 feet). The fellow who designed this marvel was Ivan Merchant, and interestingly, he also designed the long Astoria-Megler bridge that crosses the Columbia River between Washington and Oregon, which we saw at the onset of this coastal ride. Hope the wind is calm when here.

It is a very long way down on this bridge! Do heights bother you?

Image by Alex Derr (Gull's Eye Aerial Photography) of the very impressive Thomas Creek bridge, north of Brookings, Oregon.

This image is from an old postcard of the Thomas Creek bridge, prior to all the trees of the forest growing back to full size. When you ride over the bridge today, it will not be all barren like this.

After crossing this fascinating aerial structure, it is only about 9 miles to Harris Beach State Park, in Brookings, the large Oregon town that is only 6 miles or so north of California, the Golden State. There is no shortage of awesome scenery, all within easy walking distance from the campground. You'll see the usual sea stacks, huge rocks, and inspiring cliffs, with trails to the most photogenic places you can imagine!

Harris Beach is named after George Scott Harris, a fellow from Scotland who first acquired the land here sometime around 1871. He was a British soldier in India, which the British tried to rule for a while until one of the locals stood up to them. George then served in Africa and New Zealand. He finally got to San Francisco in 1860 and worked in construction on railroads before arriving in what we now call Brookings. He was a sheep and cow farmer on this state park land, and also a county commissioner in 1886. The land went to his nephew James in 1925, and between 1926 and 1985, the state of Oregon scooped it up for this park. It sits on 174 acres, and has over 97,000 campers each year.

Harris Beach State Park comes up not too far past the Welcome to Brookings stone structure. It's all downhill now. Time is short.

You get nice hot showers, **laundry**, and sea stacks here! <u>Turn</u>!

Brookings (MP 357) is the jumping off point for the California state line, with everything you could need in a large coastal town. This town was named after John Brookings, president of the Brookings Lumber and Box company. About 7,000 residents call this gorgeous southern coastal town home, a place that is usually called the "**Banana Belt**" of the Oregon Coast, due to its mild and pleasant climate (it's just right).

In 1906, a forestry man was hired to come down and assess the lumber potential of the region. Well, after surveying the mountains, and the Chetco River area, he told them that a lumber based town would be their wealth and success, and so it happened and still is today. Fortunately, the only known remaining redwood tree grove in Oregon still stands along the Chetco River, and is now protected from the logging industry! From the Harris Beach State Park campground at night, you will hear the huge lumber mill doing whatever operations it does all night long.

So, Brookings is a lumber town, with commercial fishing and lily bulb cultivation also providing financial support. Tourism is also now a large part of this town, although this southern coast town is less dependent on tourists than many of the towns we have ridden through farther north. The primary aspect of current population growth here is **retirees from California** who see it as a wonderful warm and scenic locale to spend their twilight years.

In 2011, a tsunami hit Brookings, and although the largest waves were only 8 feet, damages were still sustained by boats, which were sunk and sent adrift at the whim of the waters. The cause of this wet event was a magnitude 9 earthquake, called the Tōhoku quake, off the eastern shore of Japan. Damage estimates reached $30,000,000. Fortunately for bikers and trikers riding the **Oregon Coast Bike Route**, the state park is what we call tsunami safe, sitting very high on the cliffs at the north side of town. The harbor where the most damage was done sits quite a bit lower, at sea level of course, which is always **in the zone**.

In the photo above, yours truly poses on a chilly foggy morning next to the HIKER-BIKER CAMP sign. There is a limit of three consecutive night stays out of every 14 days. If you are in no hurry, hang out here for a bit. There is plenty of cool hiking. A short little path leads to the restrooms and **laundry** to the right.

I am sitting on the trail that leads from the campground down through the crevasses and cliffs to the very idyllic beach below.

The vista you see upon entering the park from OCH 101 is great! Everywhere here is truly a feast for the eyes and mind. Enjoy!

Who would not be impressed by such stunning views as this?

Or, how about this? Oregon's coast ranks as the **most** impressive!

See those farthest mountains? They are not in Oregon!

Here is a telephoto image that brings California a little closer.

South of the campground you'll find even more idyllic settings!

Okay, so here's the scoop on Harris Beach State Park relative to the town of Brookings. Yes, it's in town, but a mile or less from the state park entrance. This means that if you roll into here in need of groceries or other supplies, you have two options:
    1) Wait until morning on your way to the California line to get your grub and nomadic stuff to refill your bags, or …
    2) Ride on into the Fred Meyer superstore at the north end, and hurry back for dinner, a shower, and your **laundry**.

If you stocked up on grocery items in Gold Beach, this campground is pretty well equipped to do option 1, because of the showers <u>AND</u> laundry facility, which is unique to this coastal state park. They do have a **strict** time when they lock the laundry room each night, and if your clothes are still drying, you'll have to either leave them until morning when it re-opens, or take them damp to drape over your bike at night. This happened to <u>me</u>! Yep, that laundry manager really manages, to the minute! No pity!

297

When you pedal out of Harris Beach State Park in the morning on your way to California (close now), this is the sign you'll read.

The Fred Meyer store, on the north edge of town, has anything a biker could need, including a full grocery store. If they don't, there is a **bike shop** a few blocks to the southeast of this store. These Fred Meyer **all-in-one superstores** are all around Oregon, and all up and down the coast, as you passed at MP 188 way back in Florence. They even have a bicycle department!

On maps, you will see the names of two towns appearing here, one of Brookings (prior to crossing the Chetco River), and one of Harbor (after crossing the Chetco River). Maps refer to the entirety of the municipalities as Brookings-Harbor in some cases, although in reality from the standpoint of a normal human not interested in municipal boundaries, it all just seems like a big town of Brookings, thus, like most folks, I just call it that.

The final lighthouse of Oregon is found at the southern end of the marina at the Port of Brookings, which is over the big bridge (easy to cross, BTW), and on the right. This is called the Pelican Bay lighthouse, and it is privately owned. It was not one created by Oregon, but rather a lighthouse enthusiast who sought permission from the state to light up the sea here. Unlike some of the lighthouses we have visited on this journey, Pelican Bay is not haunted. This light sits on a 100 foot cliff, and was officially lit on July 4th 1999, after satisfying the strict approval processes of Oregon, making it one of the newest in the United States. There is a US Coast Guard station nearby. From this location, you can see the Saint George Reef lighthouse in California off in the distance.

The Pelican Bay private residence lighthouse as seen from below.

The final miles to be pedaled from Brookings down to the California state line are a breeze. The typically stated distance is 6 miles, but of course, that depends on whether one starts the mileage counting from Harris Beach State Park, or the center of town, or the Chetco River, or the south end of the unincorporated municipality of Harbor. This is why I recommend not getting too hung-up on mileage figures. It's no big deal. It is an easy ride.

There are two options for these final 5 miles. Either one is a snap. The first option is to take the official **Oregon Coast Bike Route** diversion, which begins immediately after the bridge over the Chetco River. This is the Lower Harbor road, and it takes you past the marina and lighthouse, and then south through the flower fields on what becomes Oceanview Drive, which roughly parallels OCH 101, except that Oceanview Drive is nearer to the water. It eventually tosses you back out onto 101. The second of the two final options is simply to remain on the OCH 101, which is the quickest and most direct method to reach California. The highway is wide, with great shoulder width, and you won't even break a sweat from here to the border. Take your pick.

Opting for the beautiful diversion is a little more work because it's not quite perfectly flat, but it provides close views of easter lily agricultural production. I even hear there are some azaleas in this neck of the woods too. So if you love flowers and lighthouses, this is your lucky day to combine both sights! The flower cultivation and sales business is a notable financial boom to this Brookings region, and thus it is known as the **Easter Lily Capital** of the World. An extra day here might be nice.

If you are only choosing to ride the **Oregon Coast Bike Route** as described in this book, I would recommend camping at Harris Beach State Park for two nights. The first, just set up camp and relax after riding south from Gold Beach. Then, the next day, just leisurely pedal to the California line, perhaps a little way into the state, and then back up to Brookings for your second night.

If this **Oregon Coast Bike Route** is but one portion of a longer journey down to San Francisco, Los Angeles, or Mexico, get any supplies you need in Brookings, and then head out first thing in the morning, as there is a lot of riding ahead of you on this day. You will be riding through the Redwood National and State Parks on some demanding grades with very narrow curvy roadway and minimal shoulder. The **Del Norte Coast Redwoods State Park** campground at **Mill Creek** seems like a good option if looking at a map, however it's **2.2 miles** down a very **old** and broken-up paved road that is **insanely steep**, meaning you'd be expending mega-calories the next morning to even get back up to the Pacific Coast Highway 101 (highway's name in California).

You will notice an interesting thing at the transition from Oregon to California (MP 363): The shoulder, which remains plenty wide and easy, becomes exceptionally smooth right at the line! From a nice Oregon experience, you enter onto a fantastic California experience, at least for a little while, that is. Just like in Oregon, the coast highway is still loaded with plenty of SHIT all the way, with occasional reprieves of easy riding now and then.

Well, my fellow pedal pusher and friend, we have at last made it to this book's destination! Thank you for joining the adventure.

You won't be seeing any more Oregon State Troopers now!

The new friendships and camaraderie through Oregon is one of the high points of this legendary bike ride. See ya' on the route ...

CALIFORNIA

For reference if you are proceeding south to the famous San Francisco Bay area, it is comfortably another 9 days from the Oregon border, depending of course on where you stay and if you take any days off. If you proceed without delay, figure nine days.

Recall how I have discussed several times that GPS is no big deal on the **Oregon Coast Bike Route**. Well, I will say that it can definitely come in handy the farther south you ride into the state of California, especially as you enter the bay area of Fairfax and Sausalito, just north of San Francisco. I have done this route without any electronic gadgets, but I did end up talking to some pedestrians along the way as the convoluted maze of Sausalito loomed before me. I even stopped in at a fire station for help, and they gave me an ice cold Gatorade. Great guys – lots of help!

The road sign above is one of the first you will notice as you pedal south past the state line. Campgrounds become sparse for a while. It's around 60 miles until the next **great** state park, which is **Prairie Creek Redwoods**. Between, options are limited.

304

Toto, we're not in Oregon anymore!

The colossal redwood tress are the highlights of California!

Not the best choice – better would be Prairie Creek Redwoods SP

If you can pedal roughly 60 miles from Brookings to here, it's worth it! There are other private campgrounds if that's too far.

This sign is just after Crescent City, California, prior to SHIT.

These food thieves are all over coastal Oregon and California!

RAIDERS OF THE LOST CRUMB

If you are going to ride the **Oregon Coast Bike Route**, and you plan on pitching a tent for overnight camps, you certainly are going to quickly learn about **raccoon** behavior, often in a manner you may find less than favorable. Raccoons are a fact of camping life. Motel cyclists need not be concerned, of course.

The average person thinks **raccoons** are cute little critters due to their adorable facial masks, which appear similar to those of cartoon burglars. Folks also find it cute that raccoons can use their front paws just as dexterously as humans use fingers. But then again, those folks don't ride bikes and live on the ground at night, so they don't know the rest of the story!

The Oregon Coast Cycling Ghost originally informed me of raccoon behavior prior to my first coastal trip. Having never had an incursion during my inland journeys, I thought he was just a bit exaggerating. Turns out, he was absolutely correct.

My story: I used to camp near thickets of bushes for my privacy, but have learned that raccoon dens are in there. Now I do my tent pitching in the open, away from dense foliage. If a camp area has unsecured trash cans, I pitch my tent far away from them because these critters will raid trash cans nightly. I park my trike right next to my tent door, where I can see my panniers from my pillow (my tent is small and lightweight, thus bags remain out). I now use **OPSAK** food storage bags, obtainable at **REI**, which do not allow odors to escape – raccoons can't smell my food now.

One night while camping at San Simeon State Park on the southern California coast, a raccoon dexterously removed two of my Clif Bars from my pannier (prior to OPSAK), by unzipping the bag and reaching in to get them! No damage was done. After chasing him off, I could hear him opening the bars in his den. So, I thought like he might think, and urinated in an arc between my trike and his den – there were no further visits or thefts that night.

A small "bear bell" now attached to the flag pole of my trike alerts me to nocturnal thieves. I have seen their footprints on my recumbent seat. I have witnessed them knocking over a fellow cyclist's bicycle parked next to my tent. Raccoons are extremely intelligent. They **WILL** find a way. You must outsmart them!

PARTING SHOTS

GETTING HIGH ON THE OCBR
(elevations of the SHIT on this coastal cycling tour)

EXPRESSED IN METERS/FEET ABOVE SEA LEVEL

Clatsop Spit (start of ride):	001 m / 003 ft
Hwys 101 & 26 interchange:	124 m / 406 ft
Arch Cape Tunnel north portal:	023 m / 075 ft
Arch Cape Tunnel south portal:	041 m / 134 ft
Arch Cape summit:	154 m / 505 ft
Cape Falcon summit:	182 m / 597 ft
Cape Meares summit	159 m / 521 ft
Largest Sitka Spruce:	165 m / 541 ft
Cape Lookout summit:	256 m / 839 ft
End of Cape Lookout trail:	119 m / 390 ft
Cascade Head:	232 m / 761 ft
Cape Foulweather (Otter Crest):	141 m / 462 ft
Cape Perpetua:	070 m / 229 ft
Heceta Head:	090 m / 295 ft
Cape Creek Tunnel north portal:	031 m / 101 ft
Cape Creek Tunnel south portal:	046 m / 150 ft
Summit south of Sea Lion Caves:	130 m / 426 ft
Gardiner Hill highest point:	134 m / 439 ft
Seven Devils highest point:	176 m / 577 ft
Cape Blanco SP campground:	071 m / 232 ft
Humbug Mountain SP ascent:	074 m / 242 ft
Cape Sebastian:	219 m / 718 ft
Thomas Creek Bridge:	112 m / 367 ft
Samuel Boardman State Park:	113 m / 370 ft
House Rock Viewpoint:	149 m / 488 ft
California State line (end of ride):	016 m / 052 ft

So what do we know for sure from all this elevation talk? Well, we know that we end the **Oregon Coast Bike Route** 49 feet over where we began – see how easy that was? Anyone can achieve an elevation rise of 49 feet, right? Of course, that is only if we pay no heed to everything that occurred on those 383 miles between the beginning and the end of the route. What a ride this has been. Let's do it again sometime – it's always easier on the second pass.

Approaching Cape Lookout summit, we're getting very high now.

At 839 feet above the sea, I am at the **OCBR**'s highest elevation.

DID YOU DO THE ENTIRE OCBR?

If you recall all my obnoxious heavy-handed hints about what was truly necessary so a human powered rider could legitimately claim to have ridden the <u>whole</u> **Oregon Coast Bike Route**, then you realize there are requirements to be met! All six <u>MUST</u> be met for a rider to confidently and truly proclaim the achievement:

DID YOU:

1) Start this journey on the sand of the beach where the Columbia River flows into the Pacific Ocean, on the Clatsop Spit, and begin pedaling south from that point? This is the farthest <u>northwestern</u> point in the weird state of Oregonia!

2) Turn right on First Street in Tillamook (after visiting the cheese factory, of course), and pedal over and around the entire Three Capes Scenic Loop, which includes Cape Meares, Cape Lookout, and Cape Kiwanda? This loop contains the highest <u>elevation</u> of the ride, at 839 feet on Cape Lookout!

3) Exit OCH 101 just beyond the Rocky Creek Scenic Viewpoint, south of Lincoln City, onto the Otter Crest Loop, for the utterly unsurpassed views of Cape Foulweather, which are <u>not</u> visible if you remained on 101? This is the most "out there" scenery to see!

4) Cross the Coos Bay bridge and ride the Cape Arago Highway out to Charleston, Sunset Bay and Shore Acres State Parks, visit Cape Arago, and then cross the Seven Devils on your way to the town of Bandon? This is the <u>farthest</u> away from OCH 101 you'll get on this ride while hugging the coast!

5) Pedal out to Cape Blanco, south of Sixes, to one of the most spectacular remote portions of Oregon coastline, which is missed by many coastal cyclists? This point is as far <u>west</u> as a cyclist can pedal in Oregon, an essential accomplishment of this journey!

6) See <u>all</u> 11 Oregon Coast lighthouses? This is a no-brainer!

OREGON COAST BICYCLE SHOPS
(Get your wheels fixed here!)

ASTORIA:
Bikes & Beyond, **1089 Marine Drive**, 503-325-2961
http://bikesandbeyond.com
info@bikesandbeyond.com

SEASIDE:
Prom Bike & Hobby Shop, **622 12th Avenue**, 503-738-8251
http://prombikeshop.com
info@prombikeshop.com

NEWPORT:
Bike Newport, **150 NW 6th Street**, 541-265-9917
http://bikenewport.net
info@bikenewport.com

FLORENCE:
Bicycles 101, **1537 8th Street & 101**, 541-997-5717
http://bikesandbeyond.com
bicycles101@inbox.com

NORTH BEND:
Moe's Bike Shop, **1397 Sherman Avenue**, 541-756-7536
http://moesbikeshop.com
moebikes@gmail.com

BANDON:
South Coast Bicycles, **805 2nd Street SE**, 541-347-1995
http://southcoastbicycles.com
info@southcoastbicycles.com

BROOKINGS:
Escape Hatch Sports, **642 Railroad Street**, 541-469-2914
http://escapehatchoregon.com
lingcod00@yahoo.com (*If Brookings is the end for you, this bike shop can box your bike and send it to your home base. You can then get transportation back to Astoria to get your car.*)

ABOUT THE AUTHOR

Triker Steve is as weird as the state in which he lives. Over 20 years of being on the Oregon Coast have altered his perception of life. Salt air has slowly corroded the synapses of his brain, thus he rides a tricycle instead of a bicycle. The patch hinders depth perception, and the missing tooth allows bad breath to escape, but it keeps the dinosaurs at bay. His books are ghost written 'cuz he wasn't never schooled. Known locally as the trike hobo, his source of income is the gold bullion only he knows how to find, because his books are too bizarre to sell. He rides a Catrike 700 speed trike when it's not raining.

A crow watches over Trike Hobo south of Waldport, Oregon.

Yachats State Park wayside is a humbling place of contemplation.

Books by Steve Greene

Bioform, Evolution Beyond Self
(philosophy of life on Earth and beyond)

Bush Triker
(guide to riding a recumbent fatrike in the backcountry)

Road Runner
(three wild adventures of a pedaling trike hobo)

The Overland Triker
(how to travel cross country on a human powered trike)

Free On Three
(all there is to know about recumbent tricycles)

Death Valley Book Of Knowledge
(an extensive national park knowledge resource)

Exploring Wild Death Valley
(personal 4x4 journeys in Death Valley National Park)

Colorado Lawman
(Law enforcement memoirs of officer Steve Greene)

* * *

Available from Amazon.com and other online stores

Steve's Amazon portal
amazon.com/author/stevegreene

Nearly midway on the Oregon Coast Bike Route

See ya' ...

(gotta' go)

320

Made in the USA
Charleston, SC
11 November 2016